Cross-Cultural
Practice
SOCIAL WORK
WITH DIVERSE
POPULATIONS

ALSO AVAILABLE

FROM LYCEUM BOOKS

Karen V. Harper & Jim Lantz

Cross-Cultural Practice

SOCIAL WORK

WITH DIVERSE

POPULATIONS

Lyceum

BOOKS

© Lyceum Books, Inc., 1996

Published by

LYCEUM BOOKS, INC.
5758 S. Blackstone Ave.
Chicago, Illinois 60637
312+643-1903 (Fax)
312+643-1902 (Phone)

ISBN 0-925065-20-X

Dedicated to our Families
Stacia and Christopher
AND
Jan and Max

About the Authors

Karen Harper is dean of the School of Social Work, West Virginia University, and Jim Lantz is associate professor at The Ohio State University College of Social Work. Both have served as consultants, trainers, and supervisors to a variety of social work agencies and family treatment centers in the Midwest. The authors have published extensively in the areas of existential family therapy and cross-cultural social work practice, and both have actively pioneered the use of Dr. Viktor Frankl's existential treatment concepts in the social work profession.

Contents

Foreword

In the past two decades or so, several specific developments have occurred in the field of social work. The work of Karen Harper and Jim Lantz reflects some of these developments and, in fact, integrates them so that they have direct practice relevance.

One such development involves the need for practitioners to attempt to enter into, and understand, the world in which the client operates. This world is not just the objective quality world itself but includes the way in which the client processes the world, and the way in which social meanings are both created and exchanged between actors and significant social environments. This theoretical development requires a corresponding evolution in the range of practice responses. To support change efforts by clients, practitioners have to be allowed by clients into the world of clients and have to encourage—say say "coach"—clients to assess change possibilities. This emphasis on meaning and change on the clients' terms is central to practice. Practitioners need to realize this and to actually help promote client understanding of meanings, the evolution of meanings, and so on. Harper and Lantz continually stress the importance of client and practitioner engaging each other at the point of meaning and relevance.

Practice issues of meaning and relevance clearly require the practitioner to be aware of a second development in social work—the growing amount of material on diverse groups in society. Social workers need to know how members of different groups process their worlds and how their cultures actually organize meanings and answers to address basic human concerns. Embedded in the diversity content of this book is a strong appreciation of a strengths perspective. Practitioners need to see that a strengths perspective can be used only if workers know the distinctive cultural packages available to clients. With this knowledge, valid assessment and intervention can occur. Harper and Lantz typically encourage clients to reflect the functional and positive aspects of themselves and their social environments.

Finally, social work practice has reflected the growing appreciation of the fact that certain groups routinely have to deal with difficult situations. Social workers need to know about these situations and the stressors experienced. Harper and Lantz discuss this interplay, especially as it relates to women and veterans and how practitioners who work with clients from these two groups choose to respond.

All in all, Harper and Lantz provide a major service to the practitioner. They directly link the content on diversity to practice, and in so doing suggest the range of roles appropriate for both client and helper.

> Thomas M. Meenaghan
> Professor, New York University
> School of Social Work

Acknowledgments

We are grateful to our clients and students for helping us to think in greater depth about human nature and social work practice. We express appreciation to our mentors, Milton Rosner and Walter Pillow, professors emeriti, College of Social Work, Ohio State University, who have helped us gain both knowledge and sensitivity for effective teaching and social work practice. We also wish to acknowledge Helene Bache and Linda Welch for their clerical assistance in working on this manuscript. Finally, we wish to thank Viktor Frankl for his teachings and also for his personal encouragement.

Introduction

In the late 1960s and early 1970s, social work practitioners witnessed a sudden increase in the number of articles about social work practice with minority culture clients that appeared in both the counseling and social work literature. Many of these articles were reactions to the profession's growing awareness that some of the traditional practice methods were neither helpful nor useful to minority culture clients and, in fact, were often damaging (Sager, Brayboy, and Waxenberg, 1972; Lewis and Ho, 1975; Halleck, 1971; Torrey, 1986). Some of these articles called for a modification of traditional practice methods when working with minority culture clients; others simply suggested that white, middle-class social workers should not work with minority clients.

In our view, cross-cultural social work practice with special populations of age, gender and oppression, or ethnic or racial minority groups is both potentially damaging and potentially useful (Lantz and Harper, 1989). Social work practice with minority culture clients does have considerable potential to deteriorate into an oppressive process for its recipients (Torrey, 1986; Lantz and Pegram, 1989). From almost every culturally distinct group or ethnic minority, sharply critical voices speak out against any attempt to undertake cross-cultural helping practice, warning against its potential for danger (Deloria, 1969; Grier and Cobbs, 1969). Such voices have expressed serious concern that cross-cultural practice consistently attempts to help the minority culture client adjust to the "status quo" and that cross-cultural practice is too often no more than a process of keeping oppressed groups satisfied with their impoverished living conditions (Halleck, 1971; Torrey, 1986; Mwanza, 1990).

Critics of cross-cultural practice have also directed their attention to a number of process variables that can become formidable barriers to positive helping outcomes in the cross-cultural helping relationship. These variables include language differences, class-bound value differences, and culture-bound value differences between social worker and client (Atkinson, Morten, and Sue, 1989). Class-bound value differences may include such variables as different attitudes about being on time or about making and keeping appointments. Culture-bound differences often occur in attitudes toward self-disclosure where the white, middle-class social worker values such disclosure and may become uncomfortable or feel that the client is uncooperative if the client remains withdrawn or quiet (Tsui and Schultz, 1985). The minority culture client may have experienced negative evaluation and may fear that responses made will be used against them. This has been the historical experience of many African Americans; Mexican Americans, particularly males according to Molina and Franco (1986); and Native Americans. For most Asians, self-disclosure is not culturally sanctioned nor is the expression of feelings in the presence of those of higher status or in group situations. For many, these are issues of respect, not uncooperativeness as the uninformed social worker may mistakenly think (Ridley, 1984; Locke, 1992). These language, class, and cultural value differences between social worker and client can trigger negative stereotyping, client resistance, and negative counter-transference feelings on the part of the helper (Torrey, 1986; Frank, 1973; Lewis and Ho, 1975; Lantz, 1978).

Those who believe that social workers and other professional helpers should not work with persons from other cultures are not without support from the research literature (Frank, 1973). For example, Carkhuff and Pierce (1967) have provided important research evidence suggesting that counselors who are different in gender, ethnicity, and social class from their clients have the most difficulty stimulating client change. Frank, Torrey (1986), and Lantz (1993) have all pointed out that giving a client an explanation of what is causing the client's difficulties is a universal curative factor that reduces anxiety which is found in almost every culture, and that the helper's ability to give such an explanation to the client in a way the client can accept is very dependent upon the worker's level of respect for the client's worldview beliefs and the cultural similarities between worker and client.

Believing that one's own worldview is functional for others can turn cross-cultural social work practice into a damaging process. The tendency of the worker to both consciously and unconsciously view his or her own values and worldview as functional and the client's different values and worldview as pathological (Lantz, 1978, 1993) is not unusual. Such an imperialistic frame of mind can easily result in a practice focus of helping the minority client adjust to the status quo. Practice toward such adjustment can produce attempts by the social worker to "help" the minority client to "give up" those aspects of the client's cultural heritage that trigger anxiety in the worker. Such an imperialistic attitude on the part of the social worker is generally not helpful to the minority client's sense of self-pride and self-esteem (Lantz and Harper, 1990; Lantz and Pegram, 1989; Frankl, 1959; Jilek, 1982).

Although we believe that cross-cultural social work practice has great potential to be a damaging act, we still believe that effective cross-cultural practice is both possible and necessary. Effective cross-cultural social work practice depends upon the worker's ability to both accept and respect human differences as well as accept and respect human similarities.

In our view all people are both different and similar. The basic processes of human existence are the same for all persons in all cultures: All persons need to eat, to have clothing and shelter, to learn, to grow through the life cycle, and to experience a sense of meaning and purpose in their existence (Frankl, 1988; Day, 1952; Lee, 1976; Krill, 1969; Lantz, 1974, 1989, 1994). These basic aspects of human existence are sometimes called "common human needs" (Towle, 1952). Although all people throughout the world have the same common human needs, different cultural heritages teach the members of each culture very different ways to go about the process of meeting these needs (Lee). Only by respecting the sameness of our common human needs and the uniqueness of our different cultural methods of meeting these needs can a person begin to become a competent cross-cultural social work practitioner (Jilek, 1974, 1982; Lantz and Harper, 1990; Lantz and Pegram, 1989; Lantz, 1987, 1991, 1993; Midgley, 1991).

Cross-cultural commonalities reflect basic human needs as well as culturally consistent processes for meeting these needs. Culturally prescribed institutions or processes of helping are compatible with cultural mores. Each culture's helping processes incorporate culturally significant sources of help or problem solving. A social worker who is competent in cross-cultural practice moves beyond assessing cultural differences and develops awareness of processes people use in meeting needs and solving problems. Such awareness is not merely a question of determining adaptation or acculturation of client to culture but is also the task of determining the match between the client's life patterns and the problem-solving patterns in his or her culture (Garland and Escobar, 1988). Relying upon culturally relevant problem solving strengths is consistent with cross-cultural practice and with problem solving in the generalist social work practice model involving clients and their social systems including society and culture.

It is the social worker's responsibility to understand that cultural experiences underlie identity and awareness of self in the world, for both clients and workers alike. As a professional, the social worker must pursue a global understanding of being and meaning in the world from perspectives of both self and client. Every culture has a process of "helping," and to "help" cross-culturally requires not only an understanding of cultural similarities and applications of helping within cultural variations, but also an understanding of the basic humanness of every human being (Garland and Escobar; Lantz, 1974, 1990, 1991, 1993; De Anda and Riddel, 1991).

Competent cross-cultural social work practice requires that practitioners grow in understanding meaning events in the lives of their clients as well as in their own lives. Openness to cultural differences, assessment of life experiences, and openness to uniqueness of psychosocial development in a client's life are lenses for viewing another's approach to making meaning of ordinary and life events (Tseng and Hsu, 1991; Tully and Greene, 1994). To enter into the process of helping cross-culturally, there must be awareness and freedom from bias so the common human condition can be promoted through informed practice.

The organization of this book includes a chapter introducing cross-cultural curative factors and linking them to humankind through ethnomethodological discovery. Various ethnic and racial groups, special populations, and populations of women and elderly are ordered in clusters merely for ease of reading from chapter to chapter. Each chapter informs the reader about the population and about intervening in the lives of people from a cross-cultural curative factors perspective. Populations included in the book are (1) those groups identified by race or culture as follows: Native Americans, African Americans, Hispanics, and Asians; (2) special populations: migrating clients, Appalachian clients, Vietnam veterans, traumatized clients, and gays and lesbians; and (3) women and elderly who constitute such a large proportion of the population in the United States.

The purpose of this book is to provide students of social work with a place to start in their lifelong efforts to become competent cross-cultural social work practitioners. Social work students must develop a deep understanding of human diversity in order to serve their clients well. We hope the book's dual focus upon both common human needs and human cultural differentness will give students a window of information on helping in cross-cultural social work practice situations.

Consistent with the strengths perspective and compatible with generalist social work practice, this approach helps the client use personal strengths and experiences as well as supports from available services in helping systems. We also hope the book will be useful to social work educators who seriously intend to integrate information on gender, race, special populations, and other at-risk groups into practice course content, as is required by the Council on Social Work Education.

Karen V. Harper, Ph.D.
and
Jim Lantz, Ph.D.

CHAPTER ONE

Cross-Cultural Curative Factors

The primary job of the direct-service social work practitioner is to help the client develop and utilize internal and external resources in the face of a problem, difficulty, or danger (Harper and Lantz, 1992; Lantz, 1974, 1989; Sands, 1991). Such a task provides the concerned social work practitioner with considerable motivation to discover treatment processes and activities that are helpful with heterogeneous population groups in a wide range of practice situations (Lantz and Lantz, 1989; Dixon, 1979).

Every culture has processes, healers, medications, and prescribed practices that enter the shared worldview of healing. It is from these experiences of healing activities when observed in the field in which they occur, and then recorded and observed again, that phenomena can be understood and shared. Healing or curative factors have emerged through the discovery of natural and sanctioned helping in the world. A cross-cultural curative factor is a treatment activity that has been discovered to be helpful in many different cultures with many different kinds of clients in a variety of helping situations (Frank, 1973; Torrey, 1986).

Qualitative-naturalistic studies identifying such curative factors are useful to the social worker because such forms of study can help the social worker learn about basic treatment methods that are often helpful with clients of differing ethnic background, gender, race, class, or socioeconomic status (Frank, 1973; Lantz, 1993; Lantz and Pegram, 1989; Torrey, 1986). So that the social work student can better understand how the cross-cultural curative factors have been identified and discovered, the following overview of naturalistic research is provided.

Naturalistic Research

Naturalistic research is a form of qualitative research that occurs "in the field," using a "flexible human instrument" to gain and evaluate data (Lincoln and Guba, 1985; Lather, 1991; Kirk and Miller, 1986). Naturalistic research is done in the field so data can be observed in its natural context and evaluated in terms of its connection with its social environment (Greenlee and Lantz, 1993; Kirk and Miller). Naturalistic research is somewhat different from experimental research as experimental research flows from theory and confirms or disconfirms theory, while naturalistic research attempts to flow from data observed in the field, with the result that theory is created from the data observed (Lincoln and Guba; Lather). Theory evolving out of naturalistic research is called "grounded" theory because it is "grounded" in the themes that emerge during observation of data in the field (Glaser and Strauss, 1967; Wells, 1995). Some authorities state that classical experimental research uses deductive analysis, while naturalistic research uses inductive methods of analysis (Lincoln and Guba; Kirk and Miller; Glaser and Strauss). Four stages of naturalistic research have been outlined by Kirk and Miller (1986): the invention stage, the discovery stage, the interpretation stage, and the explanation stage.

The Invention Stage

During the invention stage of naturalistic research, the field worker begins to develop a relationship with the culture to be studied (Kirk and Miller, 1986). In this stage the field worker identifies individuals or organizations who can introduce the field worker to members of the culture to be studied and help the worker to gain entry into that culture. Kirk and Miller report that in this stage of naturalistic research, the research worker focuses primarily upon "getting in" and "getting along."

The Discovery Stage

In the discovery stage, the field worker concentrates upon collecting data. Such data collection should be systematic, organized, and prolonged, and the field worker should use maximum variation sampling methods to obtain rich and adequate data that are filled with detail and thick with information (Kirk and Miller, 1986; Lincoln and Guba, 1985). The field worker realizes that the data collection stage is nearing an end when data collection stops bringing in new facts, new associations, and new data relationships (Lincoln and Guba, 1985).

The Interpretation Stage

In the interpretation stage, the field worker attempts to identify data themes that emerge and reemerge from the collected data base. The field worker attempts to assure that the identification of these themes has both credibility and dependability (Greenlee and Lantz, 1993). Qualitative research methods (such as data triangulation, member checking, audit trails, and peer debriefing) are used to assure dependability and credibility (Lincoln and Guba, 1985; Kirk and Miller, 1986). Kirk and Miller report that the field worker's major task in the interpretation stage is "getting it straight."

The Explanation Stage

In the explanation stage, the field worker exits the field, returns home, and writes the research report. In this stage, field workers must terminate their relationships with the persons whom they have been observing in the field. The focus of this stage is closure for all involved. The field worker should leave the field in a way that minimizes harm to the subjects of the research (Kirk and Miller, 1986). The explanation stage is characterized by "getting out" of the field in a way that is fair to the persons left behind. The preparation of the research report marks the field worker's return home to his or her own personal culture and is a milestone of great importance, both for the project and for the field worker.

This brief overview of naturalistic research has been an attempt to help the student understand the manner in which cross-cultural curative factors presented in the following section have been uncovered by anthropologists, sociologists, social workers, and other transcultural mental health practitioners.

Eight Cross-Cultural Curative Factors

Several cross-cultural curative factors uncovered through naturalistic research have great relevance to the practice of social work with varied populations. Their application in cross-cultural social work practice can aid the worker in discovering helpful treatment activities with special populations and clients with different cultural backgrounds. Eight cross-cultural curative factors to be described are: worldview respect, hope, helper attractiveness, control, rites of initiation, cleansing experiences, existential realization, and physical intervention (Lantz, 1993; Lantz and Pegram, 1989; Lantz and Harper, 1989).

Worldview Respect

The first and most important cross-cultural curative factor is worldview respect (Torrey, 1986; Lantz and Pegram, 1989). Anthropologists and experienced cross-cultural social work practitioners consistently point out that nonmedical, verbal, or psychosocial healing does not work unless the healing methods used are compatible with the client's worldview (Frank, 1973; Jilek, 1982; Lantz, 1993; Torrey, 1986). Since most nonmedical emotional problems result from social, interpersonal, existential, or symbolic difficulties, the healing method or ceremony used to help must be compatible with the client's cultural beliefs (Torrey, 1986; Lantz, 1987; Lantz and Pegram, 1989; Locke, 1992). The following case material illustrates worldview respect in cross-cultural social work practice.

Mrs. A requested social work treatment at a nearby mental health center because she wanted to leave her husband but "couldn't." Mrs. A was a 38-year-old African American who lived in a ghetto neighborhood. She had no children and did not feel dependent upon her husband for financial security. She wanted to leave her husband because he beat her. She reported that she could not leave him because he had "hired a root woman to hex me." The hex was the factor Mrs. A believed was keeping her in the marriage.

Mrs. A was provided with supportive social work services but was also linked with a local folk healer with whom the staff at the

9

mental health center had worked in the past. The healer used a ceremony to take off the hex and Mrs. A was able to leave her husband. The social worker at the mental health center linked Mrs. A with the folk healer out of respect for Mrs. A's worldview and with the knowledge that the folk healer would be able to help Mrs. A based upon the worldview compatibility that they shared (Lantz and Pegram, 1989).

A second illustration of worldview respect concerns a middle-aged woman who is a Vietnamese immigrant. Mrs. B was suffering from manic depressive illness and did need medication. She refused to take medication because medication did not fit into her worldview ideas about the cause of her troubles. Mrs. B was able to take the medication after the social worker at the mental health center obtained the services of a Vietnamese shaman who blessed the medical staff who provided the medication. Mrs. B improved considerably after she started taking the medication.

Hope

Anthropologists, social workers, and other cross-cultural practitioners also consistently report that hope is an important curative factor in all cultures and societies (Jilek, 1974, 1982; Lantz, 1993; Torrey, 1986). The more the client has hope about the power or potential for help in the healing relationship or healing process, the greater the chance that the healing process will be effective (Torrey, 1986; Frank, 1973; Dixon and Sands, 1983). Most successful healers, cross-cultural social workers, and other kinds of mental health workers understand this concept and decorate their offices or sacred huts with a variety of artifacts symbolizing their effectiveness and healing power (Torrey, 1986; Lantz and Pegram, 1989). For example, the authors of this book have noticed that many social workers hang numerous certificates and awards on their office walls. Such certificates and awards are important symbols of achievement and credibility. These credentials do help clients have more hope in the social worker and the treatment process (Torrey, 1986; Lantz, 1993). Folk healers and non-Western helpers also use such symbols of healing power to help the client have more hope in the healing process. For example, Dr. Lantz knows an Ojibway healer (called a "Roadman") who collects crutches from patients who have been healed of lameness. These crutches are shown to new clients who are requesting help in order to encourage hope.

A third example comes from Lantz's private practice. Since he is an existential social worker, most new clients accepted for service are asked to read Viktor Frankl's book, *Man's Search for Meaning* (Frankl, 1959). This book describes Frankl's experiences in a German concentration camp during World War II and how existential principles were effective even in such a terrible situation as a German death camp. New clients are asked to read this book because, after reading it, they often decide that if existential concepts can be helpful even in a World War II death camp, there is considerable hope that existential social work will be useful to them (Lantz, 1987, 1990, 1991, 1993; Lantz and Lantz, 1991).

Helper Attractiveness

"Helper attractiveness" is a term coined by Carl Rogers (1957) to mean the client's perception of the service practitioner's ability to help. Rogers has pointed out that helper qualities that clients find attractive in the United States are warmth, kindness, the appearance of competence, concern, integrity, and empathy. These conditions are well researched in Western society and consistently found to be extremely important to treatment regardless of the helper's theoretical orientation (Rogers; Torrey, 1986).

Torrey (1986), Sandner (1979), and Jilek (1974, 1982) are all transcultural psychiatrists who point out that the Rogerian helper characteristics are also extremely important in non-Western healing and folk healing. For example, Torrey (1986) has pointed out that the common belief that non-Western shamans, witchdoctors, and folk healers are "crazy" is not supported by the facts. Sandner, Torrey (1986), and Jilek (1982) are all convinced that the folk healer is frequently the most important and respected member of the tribe or village. Field research has consistently found such healers to be sane, ethical, responsible, warm, kind, mature, and committed to the ethics and standards of their healing profession. Sandner has pointed out that Navaho healers spend approximately 20 years learning the chants, rituals, and sand paintings that are a part of their healing profession. Sandner makes the point that the length and intensity of the Navaho healer's training help to ensure that the healer will demonstrate ethical behavior, integrity, and a sincere, self-transcendent commitment toward helping others. The central point of this brief review is to show that the helper attractiveness factors identified by Rogers (1957) are important in treatment regardless of the cultural context. Helper attractiveness is partially dependent upon worldview respect and facilitates the curative factor of hope (Lantz, 1993; Lantz and Pegram, 1989; Lantz and Harper, 1989, 1990).

Control

In Western helping practice it is considered important that the client learn something during service, and that what has been learned be used after termination to prevent problems in the future or to master and control them should they develop again (Frank, 1973; Lantz, 1978). In social work practice, this process of helping clients develop a sense of control is often identified as "empowerment" (Solomon, 1976). The practice of social work includes activities that help clients, groups, and communities build and restore their social functioning. Social systems are created and developed to support maximum social functioning. As power and authority in social systems change and vulnerable and oppressed groups gain control of their own lives, then do minority groups and special populations become empowered (DuBois and Miley, 1992).

Psychoanalytic practitioners help clients develop and use insight to control problems (Lindy, 1988). Cognitive practitioners help their clients learn to identify and challenge irrational "self-talk" in an attempt to solve and control problems (Frank, 1973). Behavioral practitioners teach clients to use learning theory principles for "self-management and self-control" (Frank; Atwood, 1992). Community organizers help clients learn to "join together" to change oppressive social conditions (Day, 1952; Miller, 1982). Community organizing involves confrontation, push for change, a message to the soul of community that change is needed. Symbols of cultures—songs, quilts, music, and marches bring the message to the community that an issue is important, that there is a relationship between culture and power (Kaye-Kantrowitz, 1992; Kahn, 1994).

On a more individual level, folk healers teach clients methods of mastery and control (Eliade, 1964; Sandner, 1979; Torrey, 1986; Harper, 1996). Torrey (1986) has pointed out that the Balian healer teaches the client to "pray correctly" as a method of mastery, that a Mexican-American *curandero* may teach the client a water purification ritual as a method of mastery and control, and that some Arab healers teach clients to write out verses from the Koran as a technique of mastery and control. Chung (1996) reports that in the Asian culture, ancestor worship goes on so that the most remote ancestor is linked to the newborn. The Hmong believe that through prayer and kinship it is possible for deceased ancestors to reach far to care for offspring. Sandner points out that considerable time and effort go into teaching the client "methods to control evil" during Navaho healing. Eliade has shown that primitive healers consistently use rites, symbols, and the repeating of origin myths to teach individuals in the process of life stage change to master the cultural tasks of the new stage of life cycle development. Helping the client develop a sense of mastery and control is an important curative factor in many cultures and is extremely important in social work practice. A sense of control helps the client manage the experience of anxiety (Lantz and Pegram, 1989; Torrey, 1986; Frank, 1973).

Rites of Initiation

A rite of initiation almost universally includes two elements: a movement toward chaos and symbolic death, and a movement toward new life or rebirth (Eliade, 1964). In a rite of initiation, the person going through the initiation is expected to change old behaviors (symbolic death) and then to accept or learn new behaviors (rebirth). A rite of initiation symbolizing this process of death and rebirth is found in almost every major treatment orientation or program directed toward helping people change (Torrey, 1986; Lantz and Pegram, 1989; Eliade).

A Western initiation ritual that many clinical social work practitioners have experienced is called the training program psychotherapy ritual. In this ritual the social worker who wants to learn to practice a new treatment or orientation to treatment is required by the training institution to personally undergo this particular type of treatment prior to his or her acceptance into the formal training program, or concurrently with the training program. Such a process includes confronting and disrupting the social worker's old treatment methods and personal methods of adaptation (movement toward chaos and symbolic death). After such disruption has occurred, effort is made to guide the social worker into new practice methods or personal skills in social functioning (the rebirth experience). Such a process may be observed in many psychoanalytic, Gestalt, and family therapy training institutions. This process of symbolic death and rebirth (the training program) is ritualized and celebrated in the certificate of completion and ceremony of graduation (Lantz and Pegram, 1989).

A second example of a Western rite of initiation occurs in twelve-step work of Alcoholics Anonymous (Eliade, 1964; Holmes, 1991). In this twelve-step work, the alcoholic is expected to confess past inappropriate behavior, make restitution for such behavior, and engage in specific new behaviors (sobriety and helping others) that are incompatible with the problems of the past. Group support, the help of a sponsor, and a request for assistance from a spiritual or higher power are all parts of the twelve-step rite of initiation and process of symbolic death and rebirth in Alcoholics Anonymous (Lantz and Pegram, 1989).

A non-Western example of the death and rebirth rite of initiation is described by Eliade (1964) when he reports that some shamans become healers because they experience a "calling" for the profession after a personal near-death encounter. Such a calling is often signaled by a dream and is accepted by the tribe or community when the future shaman tells the dream in a community rebirth celebration (Eliade; Lantz and Pegram, 1989).

In recent years some social workers, family therapists, and other specialists in crisis intervention have been using rites of initiation and transition to help individual clients and families who are experiencing problems in moving from one stage of life to the next (Lantz and Pegram, 1989; Moon, 1990). Divorce, retirement, and the empty-nest syndrome are all common examples of frequently under-ritualized and under-symbolized events in our society. Consistent with a cross-cultural world view, intervention must help the social work client develop a meaningful celebration, ritual, or ceremony if life transitions are to be successfully mastered (Harper and Lantz, 1992; Lantz, 1987; Tick, 1989; Takashima, 1977; Lantz and Pegram, 1989; Figley, 1990).

Cleansing Experiences

Frankl (1959) and Yalom (1980) have both pointed out that guilt is a universal human experience. Since human nature is imperfect, persons constantly experience limitations, mistakes, and failures. No matter how intense the effort to succeed, most people continue to fail in living up to all their challenges and responsibilities. The cleansing experience appears to be a universal human method of dealing with the fact of human imperfection (Eliade, 1964; Lantz and Pegram, 1989; Julian of Norwich, 1966).

A good example of a Native American folk healing cleansing process is called "sweating" (Eliade, 1964). In this experience the client is placed in a closed hut or tent and water is thrown upon hot rocks to produce steam in the tent or hut. The client is exposed to such steam for many hours, and the steam is used by the healer to help purify the client, both physically and spiritually. This water purification ritual is found in numerous cultures and appears to be a very powerful cleansing experience for persons who feel guilty (Eliade; Torrey, 1986; Lantz, 1987; Tick, 1989).

Eliade (1964) reports that cleansing and sweating rituals are consistently used by folk healers to help their clients overcome guilt, sadness, and depression. The cleansing experience is often used by folk healers in a rebirth ritual to help the person being initiated to remove the spiritual impurities of past behaviors and role performance in preparation to enter a new role or stage of life. Eliade makes the observation that in such rituals, the physical act of sweating takes on a symbolic function and is extremely effective in helping the client to feel spiritually clean and pure.

A Western treatment activity that is also a purification or cleansing ritual is called "restitution" (Lantz and Pegram, 1989). In restitution, the client performs an act, ritual, or service in an attempt to make up for a past mistake or transgression or to turn the mistake into something of value and meaning (Lantz, 1989). This activity is very common in Alcoholics Anonymous work and is a part of the twelve-step program of Alcoholics Anonymous (Frank, 1973; Torrey, 1986; Majer, 1992).

Mr. and Mrs. C provide an example of how social work clients can use restitution as a cleansing experience. Mr. and Mrs. C requested clinical services after the death of their son from an AIDS-related illness. Mr. C indicated he was having problems sleeping because his conscience was bothering him. Mrs. C stated that she was worried about her husband. Mr. C explained, "I kicked my son out of the house three years ago when he told me he was gay." Mr. C added, "Knowing my son was gay was a big shock. . . . I didn't handle it well." Mrs. C reported that she, her husband, and the son eventually reconciled, and that the son had lived at home for the last three months of his life. Mr. and Mrs. C both said they felt proud that they were there for their son when he was dying.

The couple also reported that they had been "fools" to kick him out of the house, and that they would always feel guilty about their "ignorance." They stated that they had lost a year and a half with their son because of their ignorance, and now that their son was dead, they would give anything to get that time back. Mr. C reported that he could not sleep at night because he kept thinking about his mistake.

In this situation the social work practitioner initially encouraged the couple to talk about their tragedy and their feelings about the tragedy. The social worker was careful not to give advice and simply listened to the couple until they felt comfortable that their worker had some understanding of their feelings. It was only after the social worker was assured that the couple perceived him to be an empathic person who had worked hard to understand them that he was willing to give them a suggestion.

When trust had developed, the social worker asked the couple how they might feel about giving talks about their "mistake" to other parents—those who had recently discovered their son or daughter to be homosexual. Mr. and Mrs. C initially felt uncomfortable with this idea, but as time went on decided that it was a good idea. The couple felt that this suggestion gave them a way to help others and "help turn a mistake into something useful." Mr. and Mrs. C were linked with a gay rights organization for volunteer work and were also provided support and training in public speaking. At this time they have shared their "mistake" in over 40 speeches. Mr. C no longer has difficulty sleeping.

Another cleansing experience that occurs in Western social work is called "catharsis" (Frank, 1973; Lantz, 1993). In catharsis the client expresses strong feelings that have been hidden, repressed, or denied. The client frequently reports feeling better after expressing such hidden feelings (Frank; Lantz, 1993). Many theorists point out that catharsis often results in insight and frequently is an important factor in helping a client improve self-esteem and reduce overly intense feelings of guilt (Frankl, 1967; Rogers, 1957; Lantz, 1993).

Existential Realization

Existential realization occurs when a social worker, therapist, shaman, or native healer helps a client discover, create, and experience meaning or meaning potentials in the client's life (Frankl, 1973, 1975). In existential helping practice the major motivational dynamic is understood to be the human search for meaning (Frankl, 1975). Frequently the primary difficulty that social work clients experience is a disruption in their search for meaning (Lantz and Lantz, 1989, 1991). When social work clients are unable to discover or create meaning, they experience a "meaning" or "existential" vacuum (Frankl, 1967; Lantz, 1993; Lantz and Pegram, 1989; Fabry, 1979; Bernanos, 1937; Day, 1952).

In a metaphorical sense, the filling of an existential vacuum is like air rushing in to fill a physical vacuum. An existential vacuum may be filled by developing a sense of meaning and purpose in life or by the development of symptoms and problems, such as some forms of anxiety, depression, or substance abuse. The disruption, denial, or repression of meaning awareness triggers the development of an existential vacuum and its associated symptoms. The social worker's job in an existential orientation to treatment is to use questions, comments, suggestions, activities, empathy, and sincere personal interest to facilitate a kind of reflection that expands meaning awareness and challenges the client's existential vacuum (Frankl, 1959; Sands, 1986; Lantz, 1987; Fabry, 1980). The following case material shows how a Western existential social worker was able to help a client and his family experience existential realization and meaning awareness.

Mr. D was brought for admission to a psychiatric hospital by his adult son and daughter. His presenting problem was labeled a "biological depression" by his psychiatrist and the hospital treatment team. Mr. D was 68 years old. The onset of his depression occurred soon after he lost his wife to a year-long fight with cancer.

Mr. D had retired one year prior to his wife's death, only to discover that his first year of retirement would be spent helping his wife deal with her deadly disease. Mr. D had never suffered from depression before and had no history of depression in his family of origin. Both son and daughter reported they were frantic because Mr. D had said he was thinking about killing himself. The son and daughter did not want to face the deaths of both their parents. Both the client and his children reported that Mr. D had not been depressed while his wife was alive.

In spite of the fact that Mr. D exhibited some of the classic symptoms of biological depression (such as energy loss, suicidal thinking, crying spells, and sleep disturbance), he was not suffering from a biological depression. In this clinical situation, Mr. D was suffering from an existential vacuum. He and his children had suffered a tragedy. When he was provided an opportunity to explore and challenge the meaning vacuum he was experiencing in reaction to the family tragedy, he was able to overcome his depression. His children were also able to overcome their feelings of anxiety.

Mr. D and his children were seen together by a social worker in a conjoint family interview at the request of Mr. D's psychiatrist. During the initial family interview, Mr. D reported that he and his wife had been looking forward to his retirement with great expectations of having fun through travel and cultural activities. Mr. D reported that for him retirement was now empty and, as far as he could see, so was the rest of his life. He indicated that he wanted to die so he could again see his wife "in heaven." Mr. D believed in an afterlife and felt that life on earth could not be meaningful without his wife.

The social worker asked Mr. D exactly what he and his wife had planned to do during his retirement. Mr. D explained in great detail the plans that they had made and the cultural activities they had hoped to experience. Mr. D reported that his wife had always wanted to visit her relatives in Italy. He sobbed as he explained how unfair it was that his wife would not get to have this visit.

At this point, the social worker asked Mr. D, "Is there any chance that your wife will be disappointed in not getting to hear about your trip to visit her relatives in Italy or your experience of the other activities you and she had planned?" Mr. D immediately stopped sobbing. He remained silent for a few minutes and stared directly at the social worker. He finally laughed and stated, "I always did want to be a reporter." He also told the social worker, "That is the kind of question that shocks you into seeing a good reason to keep on living."

In the next family interview, Mr. D reported that he had stopped having crying attacks, that his food tasted better, that he was sleeping well and was getting his energy back. He added, "Killing myself seems like a very bad idea now; I want to get out of this hospital as soon as possible so I can get on with my retirement."

Both adult children reported they felt relieved and believed the social worker had performed magic. The social worker thanked them for the compliment but said there is no magic in helping an individual remember that his relationship with those he loves can still be meaningful even after death.

The existential questions used in this clinical illustration were based upon the beliefs and values of the family. Both Mr. D and his children believed in life after death. They believed Mr. D would see his wife again after his death. They also believed that behavior is meaningful only if done in a self-transcendent way for the benefit of those you love.

The existential question by the social worker helped Mr. D to see that he could go on living and enjoy his retirement in a way that was giving to his wife and compatible with the values of the family. It allowed him to see a meaning potential in retirement that he had not been able to perceive previously on a conscious level of awareness. Mr. D is presently enjoying his retirement, visiting his children frequently, and has had no recurrence of depression.

A second Western example of existential realization occurred in the E case where a social worker helped a family rediscover meaning through a ritual method of existential realization. Mr. and Mrs. E were referred for psychosocial treatment by Mr. E's physician, an oncologist. Mr. E suffered from throat cancer and could no longer eat solid foods. His feeding process was considerably less than dignified. Mr. E reported that he obsessed about solid food, and Mrs. E reported that it bothered her that he could not even enjoy his food. For over 40 years the members of the E family had been sitting down at the dinner table and "sharing bread." The family had abandoned this activity once Mr. E was unable to eat solid food.

In this practice situation, the family members had always used the family dinner as an opportunity to signal, share, and experience meaning. With loss of this ritual, the family experienced an emptiness in their daily lives. They experienced an existential vacuum. The social worker's task was complex. One part of the task was to help the family create a new ritual family members could use to share and experience meaning. When the E family did replace the lost dinner ritual, Mr. E reported that he no longer was obsessing about solid foods.

A shamanic and folk healing treatment concept that is very similar to Frankl's existential-meaning vacuum is called "soul loss" (Eliade, 1964). Both Eliade and Jilek (1982) have pointed out that healing rituals performed by shamans to call back the client's "fugitive soul" help the client discover or reestablish a connection with meaning. For Eliade the folk magician, healer, yogi, shaman, and guru are all existential psychotherapists working with the basic processes of meaning and existence. Eliade reports that the basic treatment factor in both existential psychotherapy and shamanic soul loss treatment is an existential attempt to rediscover "sacred meanings" camouflaged in the client's life.

Physical Intervention

Physical intervention is a process of treatment in which the helper provides the client medication or surgery (Takashima, 1977). In modern Western society, medications and surgery are most frequently provided by physicians to correct biochemical imbalances or to repair damaged tissue (Takashima). In many non-Western or so-called "primitive" societies, medications and surgery are provided for symbolic, sacred, or cathartic reasons (Eliade, 1964). In modern Western society, physical intervention is most effectively utilized with specific tissue damage or malfunction problems (Takashima). Our Western knowledge about the symbolic, sacred, and cathartic uses of physical intervention is limited in its depth and scope (Jilek, 1974, 1982; Sandner, 1979; Torrey, 1986). Physical intervention in today's Western culture rarely extends beyond scientific application by commonly accepted techniques that give no attention to personal, social, or existential meanings.

An Existential Understanding of the Cross-Cultural Curative Factors

In our view, the eight cross-cultural curative factors that emerge and reemerge in many naturalistic studies of the treatment process are useful for three basic reasons (Lantz and Harper, 1990). These curative factors have great potential to (1) facilitate client meaning awareness, (2) facilitate client control over meaning opportunities in the social environment, and (3) facilitate an expansion of meaning opportunities within the social environment. When the curative factors facilitate meaning awareness we call this existential reflection. When the curative factors facilitate client control over meaning opportunities we call this social skills training. When the curative factors expand meaning opportunities in the social environment, we call this network intervention. Existential reflection, social skills training, and network intervention are three powerful forms of treatment useful in cross-cultural pursuits of meaning and purpose in life.

Minority Responses to a Dominant Culture

The cross-cultural social work practitioner can best use the previously described cross-cultural curative factors to help the minority culture client if the practitioner has an adequate understanding of what it is like to live in a country as a member of a minority group or special population. In spite of the American democratic traditions and stated national philosophy of welcoming persons who are different and who come from distant shores, minority group members in the United States do face discrimination, hatred, and often violence as they attempt to "make it" in the United States (Williams, 1987; Fabry, 1980). It is not easy to live in the United States as a member of a special population or minority group (Williams, 1987; Wong, 1988). The identification of coping strategies used by minority group members in the face of discrimination, hatred, and violence is important in that such understanding can protect the practitioner from labeling minority coping strategies as pathology or mental illness (Jilek, 1982; Weiss and Parish, 1989; Greenlee and Lantz, 1993). Identification of ways in which minority group members respond to the dangers of living in the United States is extremely important information for the practitioner of cross-cultural social work (Greenlee and Lantz).

It is impossible to identify all of the adaptive strategies used by minority group members to cope with societal oppression. Nevertheless, a few of the adaptive coping strategies that we and others (Spindler and Spindler, 1971; Jilek, 1982; Lantz and Harper, 1989) have noticed that some minority group members use in the face of racism, hatred, violence, prejudice, and disrespect are important strategies in maintaining a personal sense of meaning in the world. Five commonly identified coping strategies are the traditional, acculturation, transitional, hybrid, and cross-cultural double bind coping strategies.

The Traditional Coping Strategy

Traditional minority culture group members attempt to maintain their traditional values, norms, and methods of experiencing meaning while living in the middle of the dominant cultural situation (Spindler and Spindler, 1971; Sue, 1981). The traditional minority culture group member resists acculturation and attempts to interact with representatives of the dominant culture as seldom as possible. Feeling close to their dominant culture and in touch with the meaning they hold of self in their cultural world, traditional minority culture group members are not highly vulnerable to the experience of an existential vacuum because they maintain the values and meaning rituals of their past (Jilek, 1982; Spindler and Spindler). For some, this response is in reaction to the hostile world or society where they are excluded from participation (Chestang, 1972).

The traditional coping strategy may work better for first generation members of minority groups or special populations because of the recency of their relocation. Yet, many traditional minority culture group members often experience with sadness the realization that their children may not wish to maintain the traditional ways. Often this realization leads to considerable intergenerational conflict (Lantz, 1978). The traditional minority culture group member will seldom volunteer to be a client of dominant culture representatives. At times, the traditional minority culture group member will request treatment in instances of intergenerational conflict (Lantz, 1978; Lantz and Harper, 1989; Jilek, 1974, 1982).

Although the traditional minority culture group member is not highly vulnerable to meaning disruptions, he or she is very vulnerable to economic and political exploitation (Spindler and Spindler, 1971). Because the traditional minority group member wants to avoid interaction with the dominant culture and attempts to resist acculturation, he or she remains somewhat ignorant of the legal and political strategies of the dominant culture and often is not prepared to use these strategies for self-protection (Caudill, 1963). American Indians, African Americans, and Appalachians are three fairly traditional groups who have had land, minerals, and economic resources taken from them by dominant culture representatives, partially because they were unfamiliar with the legal and political processes of the dominant culture (Deloria, 1969; Erikson, 1976; Lantz and Harper, 1989). In our opinion, the traditional coping strategy works fairly well for many minority culture group members unless they own mineral-rich land or some other valuable resource that is coveted by members of the dominant culture (Lantz and Harper, 1989; Caudill). Resource ownership tends to require greater interaction with the dominant culture and may limit the effectiveness of traditional coping strategies.

The Acculturation Coping Strategy

The acculturated minority group member successfully learns, accepts, and internalizes the norms, values, and methods of discovering meaning of the dominant culture group (Spindler and Spindler, 1971). Such individuals are often very willing to become the client of a dominant culture representative and sometimes view such clienthood as a symbol of successful acculturation (Lantz, 1978). The acculturated client who has been successful in learning the dominant culture's methods of discovering meaning is still somewhat vulnerable to the experience of meaning disruptions (Lantz, 1978). If racism and discrimination did not exist, the acculturation coping strategy would be effective and the minority group member attempting acculturation would not be so vulnerable to meaning disruptions (Jilek, 1982; Williams, 1987).

Unfortunately, racism and hatred do exist. In recent years, more and more minority group members who have adopted the norms and values of the dominant culture are finding their experience of acculturation to be "hollow and lacking meaning" (Deloria, 1969; Jilek, 1982) and are returning to their traditional values, norms, and old ways of discovering and experiencing a sense of meaning and purpose in life (Jilek, 1982). Such a return to the past often results in a hybrid form of acculturation that successfully incorporates both old and new and is extremely effective in protecting the minority group member from experiencing meaning disruptions and an existential vacuum (Brown, 1981; Jilek, 1982; Spindler and Spindler, 1971). This hybrid coping strategy is discussed later in this chapter.

The Transitional Coping Strategy

The transitional minority culture group member is the most vulnerable to existential-meaning disruptions (Spindler and Spindler, 1971; Lantz, 1978; Brown, 1965). He or she is in the process of giving up traditional methods of discovering and experiencing meaning in an attempt to learn the methods of finding meaning that are used by the dominant cultural group (Spindler and Spindler). During this process of change, the transitional minority culture group member is especially vulnerable to meaning disruptions because traditional methods of meaning discovery are being replaced with new methods that are not initially comfortable and familiar and may not fit well with the individual's basic strengths and methods of personal adaptation (Spindler and Spindler; Jilek, 1982; Lantz, 1978; Billingsley, 1968; Brown, 1965).

Many transitional minority culture group members experience existential frustration, especially soon after geographical migration (Lantz and Harper, 1990). Such transitional meaning disruptions have been described in detail by Frankl (1959), Krill (1978), Lifton (1973), Lantz and Harper (1989), Fabry (1979), Jilek (1974, 1982), Greenlee (1990), Erikson (1976), Billingsley (1969), and Harper and Lantz (1992).

The Hybrid Coping Strategy

In the hybrid coping strategy, the minority culture member successfully integrates elements of the dominant culture with elements of his or her traditional ways (Spindler and Spindler, 1971; Jilek, 1982). If a successful integration occurs, the minority group member is able to utilize the legal and political strategies of the dominant culture for self-protection, yet maintain the values, norms, and rituals of the minority tradition to enhance a sense of personal identity and meaning in the face of discrimination and hatred of the dominant cultural group (Jilek, 1982). We believe that this kind of hybrid coping strategy is similar to what Solomon (1976) means when she talks about "empowerment." Examples of such a hybrid coping strategy in the United States include the black pride movement (Williams, 1987), the gay rights movement (Weaver, 1982), the feminist movement (Hanmer and Statham, 1989), the Vietnam veterans' self-help movement (Lifton, 1973), and the reemergence of shamanism as a form of native healing in the Pacific Northwest (Jilek, 1974, 1982).

The Cross-Cultural Double Bind

Many minority culture group members experience what can be called the "cross-cultural double-bind." In the cross-cultural double-bind, a member of a minority culture is encouraged by the dominant culture to change, adapt, and accept the values, norms, and methods of experiencing meaning used by members of the dominant culture. Institutions of the dominant culture develop laws, rules, and procedures making it difficult for minority culture group members to maintain their traditional methods of experiencing meaning. At the same time, the institutions of the dominant culture that encourage acculturation also begin to develop rules, procedures, and laws prohibiting the minority culture client from experiencing the rewards of acculturation. In such a double-bind situation, the member of a minority culture cannot utilize either the old or the new to create a sense of meaning in the new cultural environment (Spindler and Spindler, 1971; Lantz, 1978). This cultural double-bind has been used in the United States against the minority culture groups discussed in this book.

Summary

Curry (1964), Lantz (1978, 1993), and Lantz and Harper (1990) have pointed out the need for social work practitioners to learn more about cross-cultural curative factors and to begin to use them more effectively in the practice situation. In this chapter we have described both the Western and folk healer use of eight cross-cultural curative factors, and have also described a number of adaptive minority responses to living in a dominant culture. We hope that this chapter will be of use to practitioners who want to increase their ability to practice social work effectively in the cross-cultural practice situation.

CHAPTER TWO

Native American Clients

At the time of first contact between Native Americans and white European explorers, there were approximately 18 million Native Americans living above the present borders between Mexico and the United States. At that time, there were about 300 different languages spoken by different Native American tribes and cultural groups (John, 1988). Nearly 2 million Americans were counted as American Indians in the 1990 census. Cultural diversity among both past and present Native Americans has made it difficult to develop accurate generalizations about this population. Such diversity, coupled with different patterns of acculturation, has made it very difficult to accurately characterize "normal" cultural patterns among Native Americans. Instead, intracultural diversity and individual differences, along with the degree of acculturation evidenced by a particular client, require that social workers recognize this diversity among Native Americans despite some lifestyle similarities.

Nagel and Snipp (1993) take the position that none of the four basic processes which are generally identified as characteristic of minority and majority relations characterize responses of American Indians to ethnic relations. These four processes are: (1) annihilation—the destruction of a group; (2) assimilation—absorption of a minority group by the dominant culture; (3) amalgamation—production of a "melted" population from the blending of ethnic groups; and (4) accommodation—maintenance of cultural distinctiveness among ethnic groups in a pluralistic culture (Linton, 1963; Olzak, 1983; Parillo, 1985).

Even though these four common processes can be applied to most groups, Nagel and Snipp propose that the nature of the American Indians' response to ethnic relations is more clearly captured by the process of ethnic reorganization. In this process, the minority group protects its ethnicity but makes social structure and boundary changes. Not inconsistent with emergent and situational processes, ethnic reorganization occurs over time and in response to shifts in power and oppression and to social economic, political, and cultural reorganization. Ethnic reorganization accounts for changes in American Indian culture but provides for American Indian ethnic distinctiveness. "Ethnic reorganization occurs when an ethnic minority undergoes a reorganization of its social structure, redefinition of ethnic group boundaries, or some other change in response to pressures or demands imposed by the dominant culture." (Nagel and Snipp, 1993, p. 204).

Of minority groups in the United States, American Indians have made boundary changes which allow them to live in a majority society yet sufficient to keep their ethnicity somewhat in place. Traditional practices of extracting products from nature and bartering goods in this simple, if not primitive, economic system were reduced as reservations became a political reality. Christian and Indian religions blended for many Native Americans and ethnic dance, music, art, and tribal practices became revitalized for others (Nagel and Snipp, 1993; Locke, 1992; Sue and Sue, 1990).

There is little consensus about the extent of intracultural diversity among Native Americans. Academic research on the status and needs of Native Americans has lagged far behind funded research studying other American minority groups (John, 1988). Urbanization of the Native American family, racism, disenfranchisement, and a long-term pattern of government harassment have made it difficult to understand whether recent research on Native American families has identified traditional cultural patterns or whether this research has identified Native Americans' cultural responses to discrimination, racism, and patterns of oppression (Deloria, 1969; John).

Anomic Depression and the Native American Client

Jilek (1974, 1982) has pointed out that Native American families have been a "consistent recipient" of governmental policies designed to break treaties, distance families from their land and natural resources, separate children from families, and disrupt the family's ability to maintain traditions, language, religious beliefs, and cultural patterns. Jilek (1982) also points out that it is not surprising that many Native Americans exhibit signs and symptoms of anomic-existential depression, such as social withdrawal, a high rate of suicide or accidental death, and a pattern of frequent substance abuse.

Jilek (1982) further reports that this high rate of anomic depression among Native Americans is quite understandable when we recognize the massive efforts of the dominant culture to disrupt the natural patterns of Native American life. Pressure from the dominant culture has interfered with the Native American traditional sense of harmony with nature and inherent sense of respect for humanity. Jilek (1974) suggests that the high level of anomic depression among Native Americans may be a logical result of a policy of direct and indirect genocide manifested toward native persons by the dominant culture since the time of their first contact with European settlers.

Issues in Cross-Cultural Social Work with Native Americans

Social workers who are representatives of the dominant American culture should not be surprised if Native American clients do not trust them. Torrey (1986) points out that in view of the history of what white persons have done to red persons in the United States, it would probably be a sign of pathology (in other words, massive denial) if the Native American client trusted the white social worker in the initial stage of treatment. Other problems that can occur in cross-cultural social work practice with Native Americans include language difficulties, different understandings of the physical space that should be maintained between persons, and different understandings of the meaning of eye contact.

Social workers outside the Native American culture may be surprised to discover that some Native American persons have different ideas about the meaning of a handshake. In the dominant American culture, a firm handshake generally means that a person may be trusted, but among Native Americans, many persons view a firm handshake as aggressive and disrespectful (Everett, Proctor, and Cartnell, 1983).

White, middle-class social workers may also be surprised to discover that many Native Americans consider it a sign of disrespect to question a person in detail about his or her personal life. A white Anglo social worker who is honestly trying to take a good social history may unknowingly be acting in a very disrespectful manner to the Native American client who does not share the worker's positive views about self-disclosure. Honest and direct questioning by a white social worker may be experienced as interrogation by the Native American client (Jilek, 1982).

In today's fast-paced world, social workers are encouraged to move quickly, make an immediate diagnosis, develop an initial contract and treatment plan, and begin intervention as rapidly as possible. This action-oriented focus, taught in many schools of social work, is generally not compatible with the Native American's respect for nature, belief in the positive aspects of noninterference, and tradition of getting to know persons before working with them (Goodtracks, 1973). A social worker who is able to develop good working relationships with Native Americans is generally comfortable with a slower process that includes a positive view of silence and the idea that getting to know someone new should not resemble obtaining food at a fast food operation (Jilek, 1982; Lantz and Pegram, 1989).

Native Americans have a long tradition of respecting both the spoken word and the nonspoken word. A rich heritage of nonverbal language includes body positions, eye movement, silences, and behaviors. An absence of a common written language contributed to more than 150 tribal variations on language. Traditions, culture, and customs passed on in an oral style preserve legends and myths of the tribe. The Native American client will often place great importance upon nonverbal communication and body language. Congruent verbal and nonverbal communication is an important ingredient in effective cross-cultural communication with Native Americans (Jilek, 1982).

Native American persons have traditionally valued living in an extended family network and tribal situation (Attneave, 1969) where concern for each individual is a concern for all (Jilek, 1982). Having a common ancestor, a clan is often large, has membership rules, and holds deep regard for elder members. Governed by the wisdom of tribal elders, the clan protects its members and prescribes behavior and morality.

Native Americans often completely understand the wisdom of viewing the family system or social network group as the client or unit of attention, as opposed to seeing the individual as the client or identified problem-carrier (Attneave, 1969; Lantz, 1978). Social workers who have been trained in only the individual psychotherapy treatment tradition may not understand social network resources that can be tapped in cross-cultural counseling with Native Americans (Attneave, 1969; Jilek, 1982). Native American utilization of network resources has, however, been disrupted to some degree by the migration of many families to urban areas in search of employment and by many of our governmental policies directed at disrupting Native American family and tribal life (Blanchard and Unger, 1977; Attneave, 1969; Deloria, 1969; Jilek, 1982).

Many Native Americans believe that children are born with the power and ability to make important choices and decisions. In reaction to such a worldview, many Native Americans utilize noncoercive parenting styles that encourage the child's self-determination and that are not encumbered by expectations about developmental timing (Everett, Proctor, and Cartnell, 1983). At times this parenting style may be misunderstood as negligent by social workers outside the Native American cultural tradition. Many human service providers do not understand the value of the Native American concept of noninterference (Jilek, 1982).

Most Native Americans value humility and modesty and view it as ill-mannered to talk about one's accomplishments in the presence of others (Everett, Proctor, and Cartnell, 1983). This tradition may make it a bit difficult for the social worker to identify client strengths during assessment. Practitioners who work with Native American children often push these children to be competitive in a way that is not compatible with the Native American tradition of humility.

Native Americans often hold a nonmaterialistic view of the world (Jilek, 1982) and tend to cultivate other persons based upon their personal characteristics rather than their economic standing

(Attneave, 1969). Native Americans generally view sharing as positive and tend not to be concerned with the accumulation of material belongings beyond those necessary to maintain life, such as food, clothing, and shelter (Jilek, 1982; Attneave, 1969). It is important for social workers to avoid projecting materialistic values onto Native Americans and then viewing them as dysfunctional because they are not overly concerned with materialistic goals (Jilek, 1982).

The Native American client's conceptualization of time is often different from the conceptualization of time held by those in the dominant culture (Everett, Proctor, and Cartnell, 1983). The white population learns early to view time in a linear fashion. On the other hand, Native Americans learn a spatial view of time, in which events take place at both a location and a certain time (Jilek, 1982; Everett, Proctor, and Cartnell). The white worker who gives a Native American client an appointment for a certain time should not be surprised if the client returns for his or her next appointment but feels that "the time is not right" (Jilek, 1974, 1982).

Religion plays an important part in life for many Native Americans. Most believe in a supreme force and feel a deep reverence for nature. Many believe that emotional problems are caused by spiritual forces or disharmony in nature. For most Native American persons, religion is not just something to be thought about on Sunday; instead, it is involved in all aspects of daily life and is viewed as a part of the treatment process. Acceptance of "things as they are," belief in noninterference, and respect for nature are all elements of most Native Americans' system of religious beliefs (Jilek, 1982).

Methods of Intervention with Native Americans

Attneave (1982) points out that much of the existing literature about working with Native American clients in cross-cultural counseling has come from working with those who live on reservations and that very little has been written about practice principles with more acculturated urban clients of Native American heritage. Attneave makes the point that urban Native American clients may be well-educated, middle-class clients who will be fairly accepting of many traditional social work practice methods. In spite of this potential acceptance, it is generally a good idea to follow most of the following practice suggestions when working with urban Native Americans.

The first suggestion that Attneave makes is that social workers should try to relax and not "work too hard" at "appearing" accepting of Native American culture. For many Native American clients, the social worker who "tries too hard" appears insincere (Attneave, 1982). Jilek (1982) points out that the Native American client is generally more interested in the worker's willingness to learn about his or her culture than in the worker's display of overly-friendly ignorance.

The second important practice principle to utilize when working with Native American clients is patience (Jilek, 1982). The impatient cross-cultural social worker who presses too hard for either information or action in the initial stage of the treatment process will generally earn the client's mistrust and will convince the client that the worker is impolite (Attneave, 1982; Jilek, 1982). The worker should practice a patient, slow-moving approach that respects silence and the principle of noninterference (Jilek, 1982).

A third important practice principle to remember when working with Native American clients is to understand that there is a deep-seated cultural basis for accepting many different styles of therapeutic assistance among Native American persons (Attneave, 1982). Such a belief may help the social worker in relationship building with Native American clients.

Attneave also suggests that any therapeutic intervention offered by the social worker from a position of empathic caring and cultural respect has a chance of being accepted as useful if the Native American client follows the Native American cultural pattern of accepting "natural" differentness, and keeps believing that help is a personal process rather than a technological process (Attneave, 1982; Jilek, 1982).

A final practice principle suggested by both Attneave and Jilek is for the social worker to remain open to collaboration and co-therapy with Native American healers if they are available and if the Native American client wishes to utilize such services. These authors have reported that such a blend of cross-cultural healing strategies is often very useful to the Native American client who has accepted some of the "white ways" while maintaining traditional beliefs (Attneave, 1982; Jilek, 1982). The following case illustration demonstrates some of the principles outlined above.

Mr. R

Mr. R was referred to the second author because he had become sad and depressed after learning of the suicide of his best childhood friend. Mr. R was referred by the industrial nurse at the factory where Mr. R worked because the nurse knew Mr. R was a Vietnam veteran and that the second author had experience counseling Vietnam veterans. Mr. R was married, had two children, and had moved to Columbus, Ohio, from his reservation in Michigan three years after his return from Vietnam to obtain employment. Mr. R felt that he was fairly well adjusted to city life and had given up most of his Indian ways.

In the initial interview, the social worker did not push for information but told Mr. R that he believed Mr. R would "bring up what needs to be told when the time is right." The social worker told Mr. R that he believed Mr. R was suffering from some normal depression after losing a best friend and that reflecting and thinking about it would eventually help. The worker told Mr. R that the worker's job was to listen but only when Mr. R felt that the "time was right to talk." Mr. R remained silent for the rest of the initial interview, as did the worker.

Over the next few months, Mr. R told the social worker about going to Vietnam with his best friend from childhood and how they both had survived combat and returned home. Mr. R told how his friend was never the same after they had survived Vietnam and that his friend had started drinking after they returned home. Mr. R told about feeling guilty because he had not been able to help his friend and that "I ran out on him when I moved to Ohio." Mr. R felt especially guilty when his friend committed suicide. He didn't understand why "Vietnam hit him so hard but didn't get to me all that much."

The worker eventually suggested to Mr. R that some of the answers he was looking for might be found in some of the legends and origin myths of his tribe. The worker suggested that Mr. R make a visit home and talk to some of the elders in his tribe about some of the native traditions and beliefs that Mr. R might find of help.

It would be nice to report that Mr. R went home, heard an interesting and helpful native origin myth, and immediately stopped feeling depressed. Unfortunately, this did not happen. What did happen was that Mr. R slowly began to reconnect with his roots and native culture and eventually decided that his friend had died because he had traded in "all of his traditional beliefs for white man's booze."

Mr. R decided that he would also be vulnerable to such problems if he didn't reconnect with his traditions. Mr. R stopped treatment after seven months, reporting that he had overcome his depression. He reported that the worker's listening skills, willingness to go slowly, and encouragement to find meaning in his roots were for him the important ingredients of treatment.

Mr. R and the Cross-Cultural Curative Factors

The basic cross-cultural curative factors that the worker (second author) believes were most helpful to Mr. R were cleansing, worldview respect, and existential realization. Towards the end of treatment, Mr. R told the worker that he was happy that the worker respected "my pace and timing" (worldview respect) and that the worker was not pushy and "let me go at my own speed" (worldview respect). Mr. R also reported that the worker's ability to listen rather than telling him what to think was a big help and that this listening helped him feel less depressed (cleansing). Mr. R also believed that the worker's respect for his culture and encouragement to go back and recollect his roots was of special help (existential realization).

Conclusion

Native American people have survived their loss of land, resources and a deliberate attempt by the dominant culture to disrupt their language, culture, and values. Native American people come from a variety of different tribal groups and manifest their ideas and beliefs in a heterogeneous way. Cross-cultural social work practice with Native American clients can only be effective when the worker is willing to slow down, take time, and become open to a new world of cultural beliefs.

CHAPTER THREE

African American Clients

African Americans are considered by many to be the most victimized group in both American history and contemporary American culture (Solomon, 1976; Billingsley, 1968; Atkinson, Morton, and Sue, 1989; Mwanza, 1990). African Americans have been treated with profound disrespect, hatred, and even violence in the United States. Discrimination against African Americans remains one of the most pathological processes in American society and culture (Mwanza; Grier and Cobbs, 1969; Billingsley, 1969; Williams, 1974). African American people have been discriminated against in schools, in the justice system, in mental health systems, and in political and economic institutions (Solomon, 1976; Mwanza).

African Americans are not a homogeneous group, and there is no such entity as a "typical" African American client or family. African Americans were brought against their will as slaves and forced into acculturation. Socialized into majority cultural values and norms, yet adopting African American patterns and beliefs, biculturalism is characteristic of many. Confusion produced from conflicting values and expectations has forced many African Americans to seriously consider their role and identity (Locke, 1992). The great diversity in the African American community results from a number of variables, including simple individual differences and various levels of racism in different sections of the country. Furthermore, African Americans have come to the United States from various countries over the past 400 years (Atkinson, Morton, and Sue, 1989; Mwanza, 1990).

African American people make up approximately 12 percent of the American population (Atkinson, Morton, and Sue, 1989). African Americans constitute the largest minority group and have large numbers of old and young (Winbush, 1996). It is estimated that 29.5 million citizens of the United States are of African American heritage, and that 64 percent of this group earn $20,000 per year or less. It is also estimated that 35 percent of all African Americans earn less than $10,000 per year (Atkinson, Morton, and Sue, 1989).

African American citizens experience more unemployment than any other population group in the United States (Atkinson, Morton, and Sue, 1989). Recent national surveys report that both the African American middle class and the African American poor rank racial discrimination and unemployment as the most pressing universal problems facing African Americans (Atkinson, et al.). In 1990, the African American males averaged more than twice the 5.6 percent national unemployment rate. Joblessness and substandard employment of African American males contribute to family instability, mental illness, somatic symptoms, and increased rates of crime (Blake and Darling, 1994).

Although African Americans are not a homogeneous group or population, they do share the common "black experience" of encountering extreme prejudice and discrimination because of the color of their skin (Mwanza, 1990; Grier and Cobbs, 1969). Color in American society is not color graduation but white or nonwhite (Davis and Proctor, 1989). Minimizing the importance of race is to minimize the cultural heritage and personal identity of a person. African American social work clients frequently experience white workers who seem to deny that racial differences exist and, understandably, are frequently concerned that white service providers will not relate to the depth and intensity of pain that is a normal reaction to such racism (Grier and Cobbs). Mr. F, a 23-year-old, unemployed African American client requesting marital therapy at a community mental health center, expressed such a concern in one of his initial sessions:

> Mr. F: It's not that I think you will try to be racist. It's just that since you're white, how can you understand what it's like to know you can do a job but know that the skin color you got will screw up your chance? How can you know what it's like to have a 6-month-old kid and a wife counting on you to get the job and then seeing that "look"—the look that tells you the man is not giving any black man any chance at

all. If you haven't felt that look, how can you even start to feel what it's like to be me?

In this example, Mr. F expresses deep and realistic concern that his white social worker will not be able to understand his black experience. Mr. F is not alone in this concern. Numerous writers in the human service field report that white, middle-class helping professionals consistently do not show evidence that they adequately understand the impact of hatred, violence, poverty, and unemployment upon African Americans and their families (Devore, 1983; Grier and Cobbs, 1969; Billingsley, 1968; Solomon, 1976; Jones, R., 1983; Davis and Proctor, 1989; Mwanza, 1990). The following processes, issues, and realities have been pointed out by a variety of cross-cultural practice authorities as areas that are frequently not understood in sufficient depth by white, middle-class social workers when working with African American clients.

Duality

Both Brown (1981) and Devore (1983) suggest that many white, middle-class social workers are not cognizant of the African American adaptive strategy called "duality." Duality is an adaptive technique with roots in slavery and stems from the dominant white culture's questioning of the basic humanity of African-heritage persons. Devore points out that during slavery, African persons were expected to function in the context of a white culture that considered them far less than human. Duality was developed in this context and helped the African American individual learn to use a public self and a private self for survival in a violent and dangerous white world. This sense of public self and private self has helped many African-heritage persons to survive in the face of discrimination, hatred, and violence heaped upon them by the white majority. Viktor Frankl (1959) has pointed out that adaptive methods similar to duality were used by many death camp inmates in an attempt to survive the brutality of the German death camps during World War II.

Devore (1983) reports that duality appears and is used as a coping strategy at each "class intersect" of the black ethnic reality in reaction to the fact that all African American individuals must still face racism in the United States regardless of their economic standing. Both Devore and Brown (1981) warn that white, middle-class social workers may classify the process of duality as a maladaptive pattern if they are not aware of the process's context in both American history and the racism of present-day American society. Both Brown (1981) and Devore point out that duality is not simply an adaptive strategy of poor African-heritage individuals. Biculturism or duality is an avenue for a minority group to maintain a sense of ethnicity, a connection to cultural values and norms associated with their heritage, and yet, to assimilate into the majority culture enough to lessen oppression. Socialization in this way allows the important aspects of both cultures to be part of the individual's life. Certainly, role strains and value conflicts do occur, but it is up to the individual to determine his or her role and sense of self (Locke, 1992).

Role Flexibility in the African American Family

Many white, middle-class social workers fail to understand the adaptive nature of role flexibility in the African American family (Attneave, 1969; Billingsley, 1968; Mwanza, 1990). Reacting to unemployment, poverty, and racism in the United States, many African-heritage families have found it both necessary and advantageous to develop and use a variety of family structural forms that are often misdiagnosed as maladaptive by workers from traditional white American families (Solomon, 1976; Lantz, 1978).

In the traditional white, middle-class, suburban American family, the father goes to work, the mother takes care of the children and works part-time, and the family's one or two children are encouraged to achieve academic success and eventually to "emancipate" out of the family to begin their own nuclear family configuration (Lantz, 1978). From this traditional point of view, divergence from the white, middle-class norm is sometimes misunderstood and viewed as dysfunctional and maladaptive (Lantz, 1978).

Although many African American families do follow the traditional family form, many do not because the traditional pattern is simply too inflexible for families facing poverty, unemployment, and the high levels of racism to be found in many American communities (Billingsley, 1968; Lantz, 1978).

The African American family has consistently demonstrated role flexibility throughout its history (Billingsley, 1968, 1969). In many African American families, children help rear the younger children and at times help to take care of aging grandparents. Mothers and fathers both work when work is available and both take responsibility for child care. All members of the family help members of the extended family, and every member of the family develops a degree of competence in all of the various family roles (Lantz, 1978; Robinson, 1989). Such role flexibility is often necessary for African American families to "make it" in the face of racism, unemployment, and poverty (Billingsley, 1968, 1969; Jones, R., 1983).

Some white, middle-class social workers reared in traditional families may confuse role flexibility in the African-heritage family with disorganization and chaos (Jones, 1983). Without an understanding of the contextual and historical necessity for role flexibility in the African American family, the traditionally reared white practitioner may confuse adaptive coping strategies with psychopathology and chaos (Andrews, 1974; Lantz, 1978; Billingsley, 1968; Jones, R., 1983).

Extended Family Relationships

The African American family and the African American community have learned to creatively utilize the extended family network and kinship system to maximize support for individual and group needs (Mwanza, 1990; Billingsley, 1969; Locke, 1992). African American extended families have learned to share households, food, money, child-care services, emotional nurturance, and support in the face of stress, poverty, unemployment, and the racism of the dominant white culture (Billingsley, 1968; Jones, R., 1983; Chatters, Taylor, and Jackson, 1986). Jones (1983) reports that this important adaptive strategy is often overlooked as a client strength in psychosocial assessments by white social workers who are unfamiliar with the African American community.

Socializing Children into Extended Family Networks

Early training of children in self-transcendent behaviors teaches early concern and caregiving among family members. R. Jones (1983) points out that the constraints encountered historically by African American families in securing basic needs within the context of a racist society have promoted a parental pattern of early training to assure that African American children develop a sense of cooperation, responsibility, and concern for other members of their family, their extended family, and the community network. African American children learn early to take care of their siblings, their family, extended family members, and other members of the African American community (Mwanza, 1990; Jones, R., 1983). This early training in self-transcendence is often manifested through involvement in the African American community and church (Brown, 1965; Williams, 1987).

A Strengths Perspective to Assessment and Relationship Building with the African American Client

Weaver (1982) makes the point that African American clients are often viewed as manifesting pathology and as being deficient in strengths because of the racism in American culture. Effective cross-cultural practitioners do not minimize their own potential for racist attitudes and beliefs and consistently use the process of "looking for strengths" during assessment as a way to minimize their potential for stereotyping and misunderstanding (Lantz and Pegram, 1989; Weaver).

The process of relationship-building between white worker and African American client can be difficult because of the potential for the worker to give in, consciously or unconsciously, to the cultural tendency to stereotype the client. The worker must remember that there are many different lifestyles, family structures, and values within the African American community and make a sincere effort to empathically understand and accept these different lifestyles (Weaver, 1982; Jones, R., 1983). Racial difference of the worker and African American client can be problematic if not recognized. Recognition of differences and genuine caring and respect for human sameness are strengths that helping relationships can be built upon (Davis and Proctor, 1989).

Strengths of the African American Community

In the same way that unrecognized prejudice can cause the worker to under-recognize personal strengths in the African American client, such prejudice can also help the worker to overlook strengths in the client's social network, extended family, and community (Lantz, 1993). The experience of victimization contributes to a strong sense of community and to a strong, intergenerational family system with membership and identity connected to the African American community (Pinderhughes, 1982). Devore (1983), R. Jones (1983), Robinson (1989), Weaver (1982), and Currey (1964) have all pointed out that many white, middle-class social workers fail to understand the strengths available in the extended family network and African American community that can be mobilized to help the African American client during treatment. Such an underassessment of environmental strengths is often manifested by social workers who focus strictly upon internal reflection with the African American client, at the expense of social action and network intervention (Attneave, 1969; Billingsley, 1969; Bloch, 1968; Brown, 1981; Weaver; Robinson; Lantz, 1978; Myers, 1988).

The Black Church

For hundreds of years the black church has been a center for the mobilization of support for African American community needs. The black church has shown a consistent ability to adapt to the changing needs of its members (Jones, R., 1983; Billingsley, 1968). A strong religious orientation in the African American community has always been an important sustaining element in the struggle to cope with racism, from the days of slavery to the present time (Jones, R., 1983). Not only has the black church provided for spiritual and physical needs, it has also been a strong influence in community action programs and in the Civil Rights Movement

(Williams, 1987). Black churches have served as a central point for socialization and for social support. For many African Americans, the black church has been the most important force in the process of black empowerment (Williams, 1987; Jones, R., 1983;Solomon, 1976).

Coping under Stress in the Here and Now

A number of cross-cultural authorities have been sharply critical of social work practitioners who focus upon developmental reflection as the most important treatment process with low-income African Americans, ahead of empowerment, network intervention, advocacy, and social action methods of intervention (Ryan, 1969; Devore, 1983; Jones, R., 1983; Robinson, 1989; Weaver, 1982). Such authorities point out that helping low-income African-heritage individuals to overcome poverty, discrimination, unemployment, poor medical services, inadequate educational opportunities, and racism in the "here and now" is generally more relevant than tracing events and relationships in the "there and then." Despite supporting developmental or existential reflection, the authors believe that such reflective experiences should not replace a concern for social action, advocacy, and environmental modification (Lantz and Harper, 1989, 1990; Lantz, 1978, 1993).

The African American value system of "we-ness" offers important interpersonal support and serves as a personal coping mechanism against oppression and discrimination. R. Jones (1983) defines the African value system of we-ness as a focus upon interdependence and cooperation in the face of racism and discrimination. R. Jones (1983) reports that this focus upon we-ness is not only an adaptation to racism in the United States, but also a tradition passed on in African American families through early training in self-transcendence, that has been culturally inherited from the family's African tribal roots.

A Case Illustration: Mrs. G

Mrs. G requested help at the community mental health center because she was feeling depressed and had begun to suffer anxiety attacks when she left home to go to work, run errands, shop, or pick up her son from school. Mrs. G reported that her husband had died of a heart attack two years ago. She told the worker (a white woman with a master of social work degree) that she and her husband had moved to Columbus, Ohio, from their hometown of Atlanta six years earlier and that she had been working at a dry cleaning store to supplement the social security benefits she received for her son.

Mrs. G reported that she had felt somewhat depressed since her husband had died, but that she had started feeling very depressed and fearful two months after being assaulted, raped, and robbed three blocks from her home.

Mrs. G reported that at times she wanted to give up and commit suicide, but she wouldn't do such a thing because her son needed her. She reported that she had lost touch with her friends after her husband's death, that she was too embarrassed to return to her family home in Atlanta, and that she had stopped going to church six years ago after the onset of depression. The worker and client agreed that the goals for service at the mental health center would include decreasing Mrs. G's feelings of depression and anxiety, helping her become reinvolved with her friends and community, and helping her to get over the "dirty feelings" experienced since the rape. Mrs. G was seen twice a week at the mental health center for the first two months of service, then once a week until she terminated services at the center eight months later.

The social worker used existential reflection to help Mrs. G talk about her life and her trauma experiences and to help her become more aware of her strength and courage in the face of the tragedies experienced since her husband's death. The worker helped Mrs. G take pride (in other words, find meaning) in how she had refused to let either her husband's death or the rapist's actions disrupt her commitment to her son. The worker gently reflected upon Mrs. G's tendency to be stubborn and to refuse to ask for help and showed Mrs. G how this could be both a strength and a weakness. The worker pointed out how Mrs. G had refused to ask for help from her family, her old friends, her church, and her community. The worker used encouragement to help Mrs. G begin to reconnect with and accept support from her community. She also used linking and advocacy to help members of Mrs. G's community relate to her in a way that would be most helpful and consistent with her needs. The social worker linked Mrs. G with a new minister at her old church who was especially good at understanding the fears and "dirty feelings" of a rape victim. This minister did an outstanding job of helping Mrs. G to rejoin her church in a way that was supportive and respectful. When Mrs. G terminated service at the mental health center 10 months after initial contact, she reported that the service she had received had been "cleansing" and had "saved my life."

Cross-Cultural Curative Factors

The previous case illustrates the use of several cross-cultural curative factors that were described in chapter one. The worker in the case illustration was extremely capable in demonstrating worldview respect because she consistently placed herself in the learner role as she helped to "bring out" Mrs. G's ideas, values, norms, and cultural beliefs. The worker realized that the other curative factors could not be operationalized without understanding Mrs. G's worldview and that any meaningful interventions could only be done by starting with trying to emotionally feel Mrs. G's worldview experiences.

The effectiveness of the worker in her attempts to understand Mrs. G's worldview provided Mrs. G with an experience of hope. Mrs. G was able to accept many suggestions for action (in other words, control) and many of the worker's interpretations (existential realization) because the worker had systematically demonstrated worldview respect. The worker's respect and the client's sense of hope resulted in a somewhat cathartic treatment relationship in which the client was able to express many of her "dirty feelings." Mrs. G reported that "cleansing" was an important aspect of her treatment experience. The linking and connecting that the worker did with Mrs. G and her community were also reported as important aspects of treatment.

Conclusion

Prejudice, misunderstanding, stereotyping, and unconscious racism can profoundly disrupt the helping relationship between the white social worker and the African American client. The worker's ability and willingness to open the self to the multiple realities of the African American community are basic necessities for effective cross-cultural practice. Such openness can help the worker to more effectively identify personal, cultural, and environmental strengths of the African American client and the African American community.

CHAPTER FOUR

Hispanic Clients

Hispanic is a globally understood term that denotes persons of Latin American origin. Hispanics described themselves ". . . in the U.S. census as 'Mexican, Mexicano, Puerto Rican, Cuban, Central or South American, or other Spanish origin'" (Moore and Pachon, 1985). Composed of various subpopulations, Hispanics are the fastest growing minority in the United States. An estimated Hispanic population of about 30 million will comprise the largest and youngest minority group in the United States by the year 2000.

The convergence of Hispanic people is probably no greater elsewhere than it is in the United States. Efforts to classify this diverse group by race and ethnicity have been confusing and even detrimental at times. As in any attempt to classify people or designate a particular population group by any single descriptor, divergent terms and preferences emerge. Hispanic people have a widely diverse heritage and place great value on cultural roots.

Some view the term *Hispanic* as not being appropriately reflective of this population as a whole. Instead, the term *Latino* has been proposed as a neutral category, excluding Spaniards and Filipinos (Hayes-Bautista and Chapa, 1987; Treviño, 1987). Treviño notes that neither term, *Hispanic* nor *Latino,* denotes race; instead, *Hispanic* is a term that connotes ethnicity of a large and diverse population.

Racially diverse, Hispanics are "White, Black, American Indian, Eskimo and Aleut, and Asian and Pacific Islander" (Treviño, 1987). Considerable confusion has resulted in the United States from the 1980 census that asked persons to select one of these four racial categories. Refusing to be constrained by such categorization, Hispanics often classify themselves as "other" racial category and write in geographic locators. The term *Hispanic* is commonly accepted by most who belong to this minority group as an indicator of ethnicity or cultural background.

Treviño (1987) is not among those who espouse the term *Latino* and believes that any time a population group receives a new label, there is risk of accompanying loss and divisiveness. *Latino* is thought by some to be a less biased label and one that would standardize nomenclature for ethnicity and social classification (Hayes-Bautista and Chapa, 1987). Others disagree about the use of the term *Latino* (Treviño), and some use both *Hispanic* and *Latino* as nearly interchangeable designations (Sotomayor, 1991).

Nevertheless, uniformity and homogeneity of culture and values cannot be implied for diverse groups from Latin America. The heterogeneity of the Hispanic population is represented by the various groups that constitute the Latin American population, bicultural practices that include language and customs of more than one culture, and various levels of acculturation (Torrey, 1986). The term *Hispanic* has been widely used and generally accepted for hundreds of years; and, according to Treviño (1987), avoids regional preferences. *Hispanic* seems to be the most commonly accepted name for persons from Latin America and will be used throughout this chapter.

Hispanic Population in the United States

The Hispanic population has been identified by a number of authors as having high rates of poverty, poor education, unemployment, inadequate housing, and greater disadvantages than many other racial or ethnic minority groups in the United States (Weiner, 1983). Although socially and economically deprived as a group, Hispanics differ in many ways as a result of their place of origin and cultural variations (Sue, 1981).

Mexican Americans, Puerto Ricans, Cuban Americans, and Central-South Americans make up the Hispanic population in the United States (Weiner, 1983). This minority population is estimated to total about 23.4 million and has a growth potential that may push this group to a total of 55.3 million by the year 2000 (Sue, 1981). According to Santiago (1993), Hispanics total about 20 million. A more conservative estimate of the size of the Hispanic population in the United States reports 18.8 million, excluding undocumented persons not accounted for by the census (Rogler, Malgady, and Rodriquez, 1989). According to Moore and Pachon (1985), at least 3 million persons of Latin origin were unaccounted for in 1983. At that time the Hispanic population included about 8.7 million Mexican Americans, 2 million Puerto Ricans, 800,000 Cuban Americans, and 3 million persons from Central and South America. Recent years have brought sporadic increases in the flow of persons from Latin America who are seeking better lives or who may be looking to join relatives who have come to the United States. Others seek to escape political unrest or are illegally entering the United States in search of work (Sue, 1981). This large Hispanic population has the potential to change the racial and ethnic mix of the United States forever.

Hispanic Heritage—A Multicultural Collage

Mexican Americans

The first Spanish-speaking population to become a minority group in the United States came from Mexico as the frontier of the United States pushed westward. Territory conquered in the war with Mexico added land, oil, and gold to the American Southwest. It has been estimated that about 75,000 people lived in this territory, mostly in New Mexico. These people experienced great racial violence in the southwestern United States in the early 1900s. Having fought settlers and Native Americans, the Mexican Americans lost to those who brought railroads, gold rushes, and an expansion of the frontier. Anglos rapidly increased in number in New Mexico, California, and Arizona. Life in Mexican communities in the southwestern United States included great oppression of those who had once occupied the region under Mexican rule (Becerra, 1988).

Being extremely hard working, many Mexican Americans achieved economic security even though relocation produced severe oppression. Native customs and rituals have become less visible among those in second- or third-generation families as many Mexican American families have become Americanized (Moore and Pachon, 1985). These families often have smaller family size than did their ancestors; many families are female-headed, and many are middle- or upper-class. Many maintain a bicultural mix of language, food, dress, and customs and evidence a culturally pluralistic lifestyle. The reluctance of many young women to remain in subservient roles or to perform domestic duties in extended families, particularly domestic chores for a mother-in-law, has resulted in changes in gender roles for many men and women (Falicov, 1982). The concept of *machismo* or male dominance often softens for many second- or third-generation Mexican American families (Becerra, 1988). As the Mexican American population in the United States has continued to grow, many who migrated to escape poverty have moved away from rural, agrarian work into service jobs in urban areas (Sue, 1981). Nevertheless, the stream of immigrants crossing the border has perpetuated poverty for undereducated, unskilled, and often monolingual newcomers (Moore and Pachon, 1985; Wagner, 1993).

Puerto Rican Americans

A second group, Puerto Rican Americans, came as naturalized citizens but experienced devaluation by the majority population. Despite acculturation to mainstream society, the Puerto Rican population reflects a mix of racial heritage—Indian, white European, and African (Sanchez-Ayendez, 1988). Puerto Ricans span the full range of skin color and experience more discrimination based on color after migration (Locke, 1992). On the island, discrimination by social class is very serious and a greater target of discrimination than color. The United States gained possession of Puerto Rico at the end of the Spanish-American War in 1898 and granted citizenship to the Puerto Rican population in 1917 (Sue, 1981). Gregarious and child-oriented family systems are common among many Puerto Ricans. For this group, personal networks, extended families, congenial family relations, and a sense of fatalism are characteristics of daily living. Living mostly in or near New York or New Jersey, Puerto Rican families frequently experience severe poverty as well as gaps in education and employment skills. Recent immigrants continue to fill poor housing and low-paying jobs, while third-generation Americans of Puerto Rican heritage generally evidence considerable cultural assimilation (Sanchez-Ayendez, 1988).

Puerto Rican men and women have suffered considerable oppression. For many Puerto Rican males, *machismo* defines the role of the male in the culture as masculine, physically and sexually adventuresome, and in a position of authority in his home and extended family. Women experience sex-role restrictions early in life but value education and achievement as a means of security and mobility (Moore and Pachon, 1985). Such patterns of early sex-role restrictions are changing under the pressure of acculturation and in response to economic pressures and employment of women as well as men.

Cuban Americans

Some authorities report that immigrants from Cuba have avoided the marginality experienced by many other newly relocated Hispanics (Moore and Pachon, 1985). During the late 1960s and early 1970s, a major influx of Cuban immigrants occurred after political and economic structures disrupted their social system as a result of the Castro regime. According to one analysis of the 1980 census, at least 803,226 Cubans have arrived in the United States (Szapocznik and Hernandez, 1988). Many who fled the political and economic strife in Cuba left middle- to upper-class social status. Being well-educated and often having professional or technical skills, these immigrants mostly found employment in their fields in the United States. The Cuban population in the United States has acculturated quickly and has obtained considerable social and economic security. Dark-skinned Cubans fair less well than those who are light in color. Most Cubans are fair and experience little racial discrimination. Many are well-educated or highly skilled and maintain upward mobility which recent migrants adapt to quickly. The Cuban Americans' readiness to assimilate into Anglo cultural patterns may be a factor of social class more than of ethnicity.

It is estimated that about 700,000 Americans of Cuban descent live in the Miami area (Szapocznik and Hernandez, 1988). This includes 100,000 of the 125,000 refugees who entered the United States by boat in 1980 from the Cuban port of Mariel. Known as the "boat refugees," the *Marielitos* arrived in three stages, with the final group including many who were mentally ill, Cuban felons, disabled, and uneducated. Marielitos arrived in the United States under dire circumstances after leaving Cuba, more in response to economic conditions than to political or social changes. Their struggle for survival has continued and is marked by great socio-economic hardships. Many established Cuban Americans have been disturbed by the images of street people, ex-prisoners, and social outcasts associated with the Marielitos who left Cuba (Moore and Pachon, 1985).

Smaller groups of Latin American immigrants, including Dominicans, Colombians, Guatemalans, Salvadorans, Nicaraguans, and Chileans have more recently entered the United States and have joined established Hispanic communities. Recent arrivals from Central-South America include political refugees. Many refugees are believed to be undocumented and face hardship and poverty, even deportation. While the future of periodic entry of identified groups is unknown, the likelihood of continuing immigration is high. In addition to continuing entry of immigrants into the United States, the Hispanic population in the United States is also increased by the generally high birthrate among recent immigrants and low-skilled or low-income families, many of whom experience language barriers as well as little access to health care (Moore and Pachon, 1985).

Cultural Diversity and Cultural Assimilation

Acculturation and assimilation are processes that define adaptation to a new culture and extend to eventual assimilation or absorption by the majority culture (Spindler and Spindler, 1971). These processes occur gradually and are maximized at the point of bicultural attainment with the expectation that cultural diversity and individual identity will be protected if cultural diversity is to be maintained. The process of acculturation includes individuals adapting to new cultural environments. In the case of Mexican Americans, many had occupied the territory and experienced being exiled on land that had previously been under Mexican rule. The process of acculturation proved to be slow and painful for many who struggled to escape oppression (Torrey, 1986). For this population, discriminated against as a group for a century or more, assimilation into the mainstream culture has been a long process.

Puerto Ricans are often the poorest members of the Hispanic community and are frequently isolated by the large inner-city slums where they live. Acculturation for many Puerto Ricans begins with developing their usage of English and acquiring employable skills to obtain low-wage jobs for basic survival. Assimilation has been slow for this group as a whole. Unlike Cuban immigrants who generally come to the United States with wealth and education, many Puerto Rican immigrants experience considerable deprivation and discrimination in their resettlement (Moore and Pachon, 1985). Some lack employable skills and some experience discrimination due to dark skin color.

The processes of acculturation and assimilation are frequently used to describe how a minority group assumes the culture of the majority. The Hispanic to Anglo acculturation continuum suggests that one gives up Hispanic culture and assumes Anglo culture. The extreme of the acculturation process, in other words, total assimilation, takes place when the minority group is completely absorbed within the majority culture. This "melting pot" image destroys cultural roots, prevents biculturalism, and conflicts with cultural diversity. In instances of giving up native culture and absorbing new practices and norms, cultural diversity is not protected. The route to cultural diversity is not linear along the acculturation continuum but is a varied path that accumulates valued practices of both cultures (Spindler and Spindler, 1971; Jilek, 1982). In this desired diversity, ethnic image becomes more like a patchwork quilt than a common or "melted" pot.

Subgroups within the Hispanic population have generally maintained aspects of their cultural diversity; yet within the population as a whole, there are many similarities. Even though the Hispanic population comes together from different geographic regions, the various subgroups share many similarities in language, traditions, and values (Gonzalez, 1991; Moore and Pachon, 1985). Some Hispanics who are fluent in English prefer Spanish and will use their native language, particularly when talking about sensitive or personal issues. Many Hispanics are Roman Catholic as a result of the spread of Christianity by early Spanish missionaries. Religion is very important throughout the Hispanic population.

Commonly held values can be found among various cultural subgroups. For example, a strong orientation to family and kinship systems is pervasive throughout this population. Families tend to be closely knit, with the extended family system serving as a mutual support system for family members. *Comadrazco/compadrazco,* godfather/godmother, assure that children needing care will be looked after by persons who are part of their extended family—not necessarily blood relatives (Moore and Pachon, 1985). A common value includes respect for elderly. The hierarchy of authority places youth in a position below older family members. Sotomayor (1991) notes that membership in the extended family is inclusive of consanguinal and conjugal relationships, as well as those connected by other meaningful and long-lasting relationships. Within the family structure, the elderly are respected and cared for, caregiving is provided by females within the families, and authority rests with the male head of the family. The importance of the family is evidenced by the pattern of mutual support that has buttressed informal helpers and helping systems and has resulted in the Hispanic person's help-seeking voyage being directed toward family, the informal helping system, and away from institutional, or formal, helping systems.

Authority, traditionally resting with the male head of the family, has allowed males to define gender roles. However, with increased education and employment outside the home for both genders, economic production has brought pressure for change. Nevertheless, some women in the Hispanic population assume submissive and dependent roles with their husbands and serve as caregivers to children, parents, and others in the extended family system. Hispanic males have traditionally been seen as courageous, masculine, and providers for their families (Moore and Pachon, 1985; Wagner, 1993; Locke, 1992). *Machismo,* the tradition of the strong, virile, independent Hispanic male, continues to be valued by many. For many, *machismo* is being replaced by more contemporary gender roles (Moore and Pachon). Interpersonal relations, *personalismo,* are valued and tend to be expressed by embraces, free expression of emotions, and warm exchanges of friendship.

Respect for others is highly valued in the Hispanic culture. Respect is not based on material accomplishments but conveys honor and consideration for other persons and particularly for parents and grandparents in the family structure. The cultural value of respect places constraints on displaying hostile or angry feelings between spouses and toward parents (Falicov, 1982).

At the risk of overgeneralizing, and despite unique geographic and cultural variations, many similarities exist among Latin American families. Many have attained a bicultural identity in which they enjoy the attributes of both cultures that provide meaning in their lives from a dual perspective.

Implications for Social Work

The process of bicultural identity has far-reaching implications for the social work practitioner who is about to intervene with a Hispanic client. Sue (1981) discusses the importance of identifying the extent of a client's biculturalism as a means of determining skills that are necessary for the social work practitioner or counselor to intervene in a particular situation. Hispanic clients who are monolingual will clearly have special needs for services. They will need to be assessed to determine whether they are experiencing problems in their initial adaptation to a culture foreign to them. Sue notes that some bicultural and bilingual clients of Hispanic origin may prefer a bicultural practitioner, but that many do not. Some clients who have Hispanic heritage but who are at the extreme right in the Hispanic-Anglo continuum do not identify themselves as bicultural and prefer being viewed and treated as any other mainstream client.

Universally, relocated persons experience stress. Hispanic persons frequently experience environmental stressors such as poverty, discrimination, relocation, isolation, and language barriers. They may feel set apart by ethnically defined boundaries such as family rituals and gender roles (Moore and Pachon, 1985). Racial and cultural factors become stress-producing when combined with socioeconomic demands that produce frustrated coping efforts at the interface of personal characteristics and hostile social environments (Lantz, 1978). Torrey (1986) has identified the problems associated with acculturation as one source of psychological stress.

Cultural differences may produce perceptions, coping styles, or belief systems that appear strange or irrational to many social work practitioners. For example, Torrey (1986) notes that traditional Mexican Americans often believe in three main causes of illness—natural, emotional, and supernatural. The influence of cultural orientation is reflected in these descriptions of illness. In other words, the way a person defines the world is influenced heavily by one's point of reference. Therefore, it becomes evident that making meaning of being in the world is informed by one's cultural referent. In this case, the Hispanic culture is a powerful point of reference that prescribes boundaries within which social reality may be defined. The authors of this book believe that concern about environmental stressors and appropriate social action are essential for helping in instances of perceived stress that may be culturally induced (Lantz and Harper, 1989). In this situation, developmental reflection and intrapsychic exploration may serve to immobilize clients who are experiencing stress and strain in coping with cross-cultural demands (Lantz and Harper, 1990).

Within the Hispanic population, Mexican Americans are not likely to seek help from Anglo psychiatrists, social workers, or counselors (Moore and Pachon, 1985). Torrey (1986) cites various studies suggesting that costs, language barriers, and help-seeking voyages within extended family networks serve to delay or prevent utilization of formal, mainstream psychotherapeutic services. Torrey (1986) proposes that culturally linked healers, such as *curanderas* and spiritualists, are familiar helpers to many Mexican Americans. Culturally congruent and consistent with the religiosity of this population, particularly for those who are not biculturally acclimated, spiritual healers help their clients fill an existential vacuum resulting from living in the middle of a dominant culture. For others, more traditional helping networks need to be especially sensitive to strains produced by cross-cultural life experiences. Again, the eight interventions that we believe to be particularly effective with clients experiencing cross-cultural meaning disruption and existential depression are: worldview respect, hope, helper attractiveness, control, rites of initiation, cleansing, existential realization, and physical intervention (Lantz and Harper, 1990; Lantz and Pegram, 1989).

Ms. L: A Case Illustration

Ms. L is of second-generation Mexican American heritage. At the time of her first encounter with her major university professor, an Anglo, she was 21 years old and a college freshman planning to major in social work. Ms. L was experiencing problems in pursuing her life course in opposition to her family of origin. The youngest of six children, Ms. L had four sisters and one brother. Her father had died when she was 19 and now Ms. L lived with her mother and brother. Her family continued to follow a traditional hierarchy of authority and now her brother was the dominant figure in her family. Ms. L tearfully expressed her fear that her brother would make her leave college if he found out that she had enrolled.

Ms. L's parents had picked vegetables in the southwestern United States and had traveled with the crops at harvest time as far north as Canada. Ms. L recalled having been in many elementary schools, picking tomatoes, living in a number of shacks in the summer months, and the celebration by her family when her father was hired as a laborer in a factory in the midwestern United States. She was happy that she had not had to change schools since the ninth grade.

Although bilingual, Ms. L rarely spoke in Spanish. She expressed anger toward her brother because of his attempts to "be my father and run my life." Ms. L explained that her brother wanted her to stay at home to care for their mother, do housework, and cook for him and his friends. She adamantly stated that she would "cook no Mexican foods for those bums!"

Network intervention was used with Ms. L to aid her in her entry to the social work program. She was encouraged to join the student social work organization and was introduced to two other Hispanic students—one Puerto Rican and the other Mexican American. She attended an orientation to the women's center on campus where she eventually joined an assertiveness training group along with several of her Anglo friends.

Personal and professional milestones marked Ms. L's progress in college, but she continued to mourn the loss of her brother's friendship. Reflection experiences and opportunities were used to help Ms. L restore a sense of belonging and respect from her family. She described herself as "cheap and unthankful," a "sister shunned by my brother." When asked whether her brother had stopped talking to her, Ms. L paused before replying, "I have been so mad at his ugly face that I forget to ask him anything." Ms. L was able to accept the challenge to speak with her brother. She had her brother meet with her in the presence of the family priest, and there they found a way to share hurt feelings and concerns for each other.

Ms. L began to enjoy her renewed sense of belonging in her family and relished the respect she received from her relatives for her accomplishments as a student. She began volunteering in a preschool attended by Hispanic youngsters where she helped them with new words and read to them from storybooks by Hispanic and Anglo writers. She helped the youngsters bridge the two main cultures in their lives, an accomplishment she, too, was achieving.

Her new sense of meaning and direction was evident the day she walked into the first author's office and announced that she would show the school how to make money for the student organization. She had decided to organize a "Mexican bake sale" and to have no more "pale Anglo cookies."

Ms. L had gained a renewed sense of meaning and respect for her Hispanic heritage. At her graduation, she was flanked by her mother, four sisters, four brothers-in-law, six nieces and nephews, her boyfriend, and her brother. All applauded her success. She was especially proud of her brother's congratulations and attentiveness.

Ms. L and the Curative Factors

In this practice situation it is important to note that the helping social worker was not acting in the role of a clinical social worker but as a social work educator. Still, the social worker's relationship with Ms. L did include many of the cross-cultural curative factors presented in this book.

The first cross-cultural curative factor manifested by the social worker was worldview respect. The social worker tried hard to respect both the Hispanic heritage of Ms. L and her anger at elements of her Hispanic heritage. At her graduation Ms. L reported that she was grateful that the social worker was able to accept both her heritage and her own differences with her own heritage (worldview respect). Ms. L reported that the social worker's listening skills helped her to get things off her chest (cleansing) and that the linking and network intervention activities had helped her feel more power (control). Ms. L also reported that the social worker's insistence that it was possible both to keep your relationship with your family and to respect yourself was extremely helpful (existential realization).

Summary

The term "Hispanic people" refers to a wide and rich group of people that includes great differences and many different strengths. Cross-cultural social work practice with Hispanic people must include an awareness of both differences and heterogeneity and should also be practiced from a stance of openness, willingness to learn, and a basic confidence in the cross-cultural curative factors as methods to be used in successful helping.

CHAPTER FIVE

Asian Clients

In recent years an increasing number of social work practitioners find that Asian clients request social work and mental health services on a more frequent basis, even though such help is not always the first option chosen to relieve stress and emotional pain (Ho, 1990; Lee and Saul, 1987). The less recent a group's history of immigration, the greater the acculturation, including group members' utilization of systems of helping commonly available to most families. Berg and Jaya (1993) note that Asian Americans are more likely to migrate for higher quality of living and education than to escape poverty like many other immigrants. Atkinson, Morton, and Sue (1989) report that the Asian American population has doubled since 1970 and now constitutes about 2 percent of the total population of the United States. They further estimate that there are approximately 806,000 Chinese Americans, 701,000 Japanese Americans, 355,000 Korean Americans, and about 400,000 Asian Americans from Vietnam and Cambodia.

Asian Americans have tended to underutilize social work, mental health, and counseling services (Sue, 1981). Part of this underutilization may be reactive to the dominant American community's inaccurate belief that Asian Americans are a "problem free" group not in need of such services. Part of the Asian population's underutilization of services may be a reaction to the cultural tendency in some Asian groups to view the self with shame when confronted with the manifestation of an emotional problem or psychiatric symptom (Brower, 1980). The worker familiar with Asian Americans knows that reframing the problem positively will help the Asian American client "save face" and retain a sense of dignity rather than shame. The great emotional distress of many Asian Americans comes from feeling shame or dishonor and not guilt, as is typical of the American client (Berg and Jaya, 1993; Berg and Miller, 1992).

The social worker who wishes to facilitate an acceptance of service opportunities among Asian American groups should have a basic understanding of the cultural elements within these various cultural groups (Sue, 1981). Asian American families have been said to be "like all other families, like some other families, and like no other families" (Hardy, 1990, p. 32). Honor, dignity, meditation, family honor, hierarchy of levels in families and businesses, good of family and not self, and experience and wisdom are valued in Asian cultures. These need to be understood by the social worker if intervention is to be even minimally helpful to these Eastern people with origins in this geographically and ethnically heterogeneous population. (Berg and Jaya, 1993; de Shazer, 1991).

The Korean American Client

Traditional Korean culture has been strongly influenced by the Confucian philosophical tradition (Lee and Saul, 1987). The Confucian philosophy of life is concerned with life in this world rather than life after death. Confucius gave many principles for living that are directed toward the development of harmonious social relationships. Five categories of social relationships, outlining the duties and obligations of each individual in society, form the foundation of Confucius's teaching. These categories include the social relations between parents and children, king and subjects, husband and wife, older children and younger children, and between friends (Osgood, 1951). The philosophy of Confucianism is especially important for understanding the Korean American family because three of these five social relationship categories involve the family (Min, 1988).

Although Confucius taught that parents and children should treat each other with benevolence, in the Korean culture this concept has often been understood to mean that children should demonstrate deep respect and obedience toward their parents (Min, 1988). As a result, the traditional Korean family encourages respect and compliance with parental authority throughout a person's life.

Confucius emphasized a clear role differentiation between husband and wife, and this principle has led to a system of patriarchy in the general Korean culture (Osgood, 1951; Min, 1988). In traditional Korean society, the husband is considered the breadwinner and decision-maker in the family, with authority over the wife and children.

In traditional Korean culture, sons were considered more valuable than daughters, while older children were considered to have more authority and power than younger children (Min, 1988). Such a structured system of authority has probably curtailed manifested family conflict, but may be the dynamic behind an increased level of reported somatic complaints by family members who lack power in the Korean American family (Lee and Saul, 1987).

Lee and Saul report that the Korean American family is experiencing more and more intergenerational conflict as Korean families attempt to assimilate into the dominant American culture. Min and Lee and Saul agree that it is important for the helping professional to determine the degree of assimilation manifested by the Korean American client in order to assess the potential for intergenerational conflict within the Korean American family.

Lee and Saul make the important point that each Korean American family is in a different stage of transition and assimilation, ranging from the conventional, paternalistic, authoritarian Korean family to a more "Americanized" egalitarian, nuclear family. If the Korean American client family is a traditional Korean family, there may be a clash of values between the family and the often liberal values and attitudes of the modern social worker. Such a clash may reduce the Korean American family's opportunities to utilize existing services for family growth and development (Lee and Saul). The family-centered Korean client may find seeking help outside the family to be extremely difficult and may evidence shame and guilt for publicly expressing personal problems. It is rare for the presenting problem to be the problem of greatest importance in situations of Korean clients (Locke, 1992). Informal dominant cultural practices are typically approached with a sense of mistrust and unfamiliarity. Trust, respect, and positive regard are all extremely important in building relationships with Korean Americans.

The Chinese American Client

Chinese people have migrated for more than two thousand years and a large number have been living in the United States for more than 130 years (Wong, 1988). Although Wong points out that family life is a central issue for most Chinese Americans, there is no typical Chinese American family, just as there is no typical Asian American family. Wong believes that there are a number of different "ideal types" of Chinese families living in the United States and that an understanding of these types may help the human services professional who plans to work with Chinese American clients.

The first ideal type of Chinese American family described by Wong (1988) is the traditional Chinese family. He points out that the traditional Chinese family includes immediate family members and also the extended kinship group and clan members. This kind of Chinese American family is patriarchal, with clearly defined roles and with male family members in the most dominant roles (Wong; Hsu, 1970). Females are relegated to a subordinate position and are expected to obey their husbands and their husband's parents. The traditional Chinese family is also patrilocal in that the married couple lives with the husband's parents. Because of this pattern, the traditional Chinese family is also often an extended family in which many generations and their offspring live under one roof (Wong, 1988). This traditional pattern is becoming less frequent as Chinese families become assimilated into American culture.

Although the traditional Chinese family pattern prevails in the United States, some of the traditional cultural values have been maintained to a greater or lesser degree by many Chinese American families. Such values and traditions include: an obligation of male children to care for aging parents in exchange for patrilineal property descent; ancestor worship; the value of filial piety (which is a system of mutual respect to those of equal status and reverence toward elders and leaders); the values of duty and obligation; the importance of family name; and the idea that marriage is a family concern rather than a private matter between two persons in love (Wong, 1988).

The second kind of Chinese American family described by Wong (1988) is called the "split household" Chinese American family. This kind of family developed in the early period of Chinese migration to the United States when male family members would come to the United States without their wives for work opportunities and would send earnings back to their families in China. Chinese workers mined gold in California and eventually settled up the coastline where Chinese people continue to live in high concentrations (Locke, 1992).

Beginning in the 1920s and 1930s, a sizable second generation of Chinese Americans had settled in the United States and started small businesses, such as laundries, grocery stores, restaurants, and other small enterprises. Wong (1988) reports that in this period, Chinese American families started to become what may be called the "small producer." In this type of family, all family members, including the children, worked in the family business. Such family businesses were often successful because they were labor intensive, with all family members putting in very long hours (Wong, 1988). In this kind of family, there was no clear demarcation between work and family life. Kinship and hard work were strongly valued, and independent children were viewed as ungrateful children (Sue, 1981). The family developed the value of collectivity over the value of the individual. Wives and children developed a higher level of status in this family form than had been the case in the traditional Chinese family.

Another kind of Chinese American family described by many authorities may be called the "present-day" Chinese American family (Wong, 1988; Hsu, 1970). This family often maintains a small business and tends to live in a major Chinese community, such as Chinatown in New York City. White-collar Chinese American families have evolved out of Chinese American families with small businesses and these families have used education to develop a white-collar or professional standard of life. According to M. Wong, such families often move away from the larger Chinese American communities to settle in the suburbs and are less resistant to the process of acculturation.

Following the philosophy of Confucianism, ethical and moral practices characterize many traditional Chinese families in their relationships at home and at work. Beliefs regarding ancestral spirits, various gods, and eternal life were influenced in Buddhist and Taoist religions which, although mixed with Christianity to some extent, are still represented in many Chinese celebrations and holidays (Bonavia, 1980).

Understanding the extent of a Chinese American's acculturation is important in understanding the importance of structure and emotional restraints among traditional Chinese who are best approached formally and logically. For those with greater resistance to their heritage and, yet, experiencing difficulty in the acculturation process, much greater understanding of the culture and ability to build acceptance and relationships are necessary on the part of the social worker (Locke, 1992; Sue and Sue, 1990).

The Japanese American Client

Kitano (1988) reports that there are presently three generations of Japanese American families living in the United States. These are called the Issei (first generation), Nisei (second generation), and Sansei (third generation). In the 1890s, Issei Japanese started immigrating to the West Coast of the United States from Hawaii. Most of the original Issei are now deceased or are in retirement. The Issei Japanese Americans found employment in occupations that called for hard work, little capital, and a minimal ability to speak English. They worked in canneries, in fishing and logging camps, in mines, and in agriculture. They faced intense racism as well as few social and economic opportunities in the American mainstream (Kitano).

Most Issei Japanese turned to their homeland for wives and were assisted in their attempts to begin a family in the United States by relatives and friends in Japan or Hawaii. A common practice in selecting a bride was through an exchange of photographs. This practice was called finding a "picture bride." As a result of turning toward Hawaii or Japan to find a wife, family life for the Issei in America was a continuation of the traditional family life in Japan. Family and kin were closely involved in all steps of marriage, and it was a rare Issei who married without parental approval (Kitano, 1988). This traditional family life included the view of Japanese society as one large family in which

family norms were reinforced by the ethnic community, a patriarchal form of family living, a system of family inheritance that
assured that property and power went to the eldest son, and a
high value placed upon family customs and family celebrations
(Miyamoto, 1939). Issei Japanese have cherished their culture and
resisted acculturation in a country so different from that of their
homeland (Locke, 1992).

The Nisei generation of Japanese Americans is now entering
late adult life and facing questions of health, aging, and retirement. The Nisei is the generation that was forced to live in concentration camps while America was at war with Japan. Many
Nisei are strongly patriotic because they feel a need to continu-
ously prove that they are "good Americans" in reaction to their
concentration camp experiences. Many of the Nisei generation
were eventually able to obtain a good education and to keep a
focus upon their Japanese traditions while adapting to the culture
of the United States (Kitano, 1988). Raised by the Issei generation, Nisei Japanese Americans who have achieved high socioeconomic success have acculturated quickly and have weakened their
ties to their ethnic background (Tomine, 1991).

The biggest change between the Issei and Nisei generations occurred in marital and family life. The Nisei generation manifested
a belief in choice in the selection of a spouse, a priority upon
romantic love, a priority on the conjugal bond over the filial
bond, greater equality between the sexes, and greater communication between the spouses (Kitano, 1988).

The Sansei is the younger generation of Japanese Americans
who were born in the United States and who are products of both
their Japanese heritage and exposure to American culture. The
Sansei culture may be understood as a product of acculturation,
and Sansei Japanese Americans may be more like modern Americans than like their Japanese ancestors (Kitano, 1988).

Japanese Americans value family and avoid displaying feelings
and family problems to those outside the family so as not to bring
shame to their family. Modesty, restraint, sensitivity, and status
in family, caste, class, and gender are powerful influences. Arts,
education, and economic success are important to many. For
many Japanese, accepting treatment or help creates feelings of
guilt and failure. Social work and other helping interventions

with Japanese Americans require a great deal of understanding of their culture and their experiences, practical and useful assistance, recognition of their heritage, and a discussion and exchange of information and solutions for problem solving (Sue and Sue, 1990; Locke, 1992).

The Southeast Asian American Client

Since 1975, numerous Southeast Asian refugees have fled their home countries for political and socioeconomic reasons, and many have resettled in the United States. Others are still living in refugee camps, waiting to come to the United States. These people are survivors of numerous and severe traumas. Many have been victims of political repression and governmental harassment. Many have been threatened, beaten, and tormented in reeducation camps. They often have witnessed loved ones being killed and often have faced death themselves (Kinzie and Fleck, 1987). They have suffered numerous losses in terms of loved ones, their homeland, status, identity, previous lifestyle, religious beliefs, self-esteem, supporting networks, and affectional ties. Many have been overwhelmed by feelings of guilt as their escape forced them to give up their homeland and leave some family members and friends behind, literally in order to survive (Bromley, 1987; Kinzie and Fleck; Weiss and Parish, 1989). In addition to these losses and the horrors of war, many Southeast Asian refugees have also experienced near-death situations such as inadequate food and water on the boat or in the camps, being attacked by pirates in their flight to freedom, tension and conflicts with other refugees or with authorities, rape, persecution, and witnessing others killed during their escape (Tobin and Friedman, 1983).

After great hardship, emotional distress, and extreme anxiety about their future, many Southeast Asian refugees who had high expectations of a better life in their potential host country arrived in the United States only to discover further problems brought about by the process of resettlement. These refugees face not only the stress of adapting to American ways but also basic survival issues such as inadequate housing, financial hardship, and unemployment (Bromley, 1987; Timberlake and Cook, 1984). Other issues in the resettlement of Southeast Asians that are most often cited in the literature concerning these refugees include survivor's guilt and a sense of obligation to rescue the family members left behind, a radical adjustment of roles within the family, intergenerational conflicts caused by differential acculturation because of age differences, and social misunderstandings between the refugees and members of the dominant culture (Bromley; Kinzie and Fleck, 1987; Timberlake and Cook; Tobin and Friedman, 1983; Weiss and Parish, 1989). Dislocation and resettlement have been extremely traumatic experiences for many Southeast Asian refugees (Weiss and Parish; Torrey, 1988).

Because of the cumulative traumas of war, flight, persecution, refugee camps, and resettlement, Southeast Asian refugees have been found to be increasingly vulnerable to mental health problems and psychiatric difficulties (Weiss and Parish, 1989). Many resettling Southeast Asian refugees have been reported to be suffering from acute anxiety (Weiss and Parish); major depression (Kinzie and Fleck, 1987; Tobin and Friedman, 1983); paranoia (Tobin and Friedman); insomnia; recurring nightmares; intrusive thoughts; anorexia and weight loss; loss of memory and concentration; headaches; emotional numbing; conscious avoidance of memories of the past; suicidal thoughts; alienation, social disorganization, and social isolation (Weiss and Parish). Very often a constellation of such problems or symptoms is present in the Southeast Asian refugee. Some authorities suggest that these cases not be classified according to their dominant symptom, but as a malady reflective of the problem constellation—"trauma syndrome," "survivor syndrome," or "stress response syndrome" (Tobin and Friedman; Lantz, 1974, 1993; Lantz and Lantz, 1991).

There have also been reports of "sudden death syndrome" among Southeast Asian refugees in the United States (Tobin and Friedman, 1983). There are a number of cases in which apparently healthy male refugees went to bed feeling well, only to die suddenly in their sleep with no probable cause of death established in the autopsies. In many of these cases there are reports that a shortness of breath or labored breathing, screams, and tossing in bed immediately preceded death. Tobin and Friedman suggest that such sudden deaths may be an unconscious suicide triggered by a loss of self-respect and the will to live. Such speculation is based on the phenomenon that many Southeast Asian refugees tend to express their trauma and survivor's guilt in nightmares of spiritual attack, the physiological effects of which are similar to the symptoms of the sudden death syndrome preceding the death, such as shortness or loss of breath. That is to say, many of those who reported nightmares of spiritual attack are possible survivors of sudden death syndrome (Tobin and Friedman). This may explain why sudden death syndrome occurs almost exclusively in male refugees. Southeast Asian men are susceptible to such feelings of guilt, since in their culture it is the man's role to protect his family and homeland (McQuade, 1989). It should be noted that a lack of sensitivity in the host culture to the emotional conflicts experienced by resettling refugees can also intensify feelings of loss and guilt, because many Southeast Asian refugees perceive resettlement problems as a form of punishment for their survival and escape.

In examining the life experiences of Southeast Asian refugees, the social work practitioner should look at problematic events before, during, and after their flight to America. These could include the horrors of war; brutal persecution under a ruthless regime; physical assaults and threats to life; the loss of one's country, family, and friends; danger and constant fear of capture during escape; anxiety about the future; tension and fear in the internment camps; and the intense cultural confusion experienced in resettlement in the United States (Bromley, 1987; Schanberg, 1980). The traumatic experiences of these hazardous events may trigger a disruption in the refugees' most familiar ways of discovering and experiencing meaning, producing a meaning vacuum that is often filled by psychiatric symptoms (Lantz and Harper, 1990). For many Southeast Asian refugees, problems in the "here and now" could precipitate repressed emotional pain about trauma and terror in the past. For example, loss of a job may remind an individual of past losses in terms of family, status, homeland, social support systems, and lifestyle. News, newspaper articles, or even movies about wars or the refugee's home country may stimulate the recall of past events that could result in the manifestation of flashback symptoms. Letters from relatives left behind or still in refugee camps and news of family and friends may prompt memories, flashbacks, fears, guilt, or shame. Communication barriers and cultural conflicts in the United States may produce misunderstanding, which may, in turn, trigger a sense of rejection, social withdrawal, depression, and anxiety attacks (Lantz and Lantz, 1991).

Mr. I: A Case Illustration

Mr. I was referred to a community mental health social worker for clinical services by his sponsoring American host family and by his caseworker at a local resettlement agency. Mr. I was referred because he was experiencing anxiety attacks, night terrors, and because he had expressed thoughts of suicide to both his caseworker and his host family. Mr. I had gone to a different mental health center six months earlier, but had stopped going because he felt that the mental health worker at that center did not understand his problems which had worsened." Mr. I had come to the United States after escaping from the Khmer Rouge holocaust in Cambodia. He lost his father, mother, wife, and son in a Khmer Rouge work (death) camp prior to his escape. He did not know whether his two brothers were alive. He had lived in a refugee camp for three years before coming to the United States. He was working as a waiter in an oriental restaurant and was attending night school to improve his English.

Mr. I was seen by a social worker at the mental health center for psychotherapy to discuss his anxiety and conflicts. The worker used a reflection orientation to social work practice in which Mr. I was helped to reflect on his own words and explore his description of anxiety and depression. Mr. I was also provided network intervention services at the resettlement agency to maximize his opportunities in his new country and to help him make use of these opportunities.

During Mr. I's treatment sessions with the social worker at the mental health center, he eventually expressed his belief that he had no right to be alive. Mr. I felt that since his family had been killed, he should also be dead. He was unable to see his good fortune in surviving, since all of the persons whom he loved had not survived. Mr. I said that he had stopped going to the previous mental health center because the worker could not understand "why I am bad and evil." Mr. I reported that he wanted to find a reason to stay alive, but had little hope that such a reason could be found.

Existential realization experiences were used to help Mr. I discover and experience a number of meaningful opportunities in his life. Although the mental health worker did not agree with Mr. I that life was meaningless, the worker did agree that Mr. I's continued existence probably depended upon discovering meaningful activities, goals, and tasks that he should do that would honor his dead family, ancestors, and friends. Mr. I accepted that his life could have meaning if he found a way to give to the world "in honor of" his dead family, friends, and ancestors.

Mr. I continued treatment with the mental health social worker for some time during which the worker used existential reflection and cleansing activities to help Mr. I find a sense of meaning and purpose in life and in his survival despite the tragedy, trauma, and terror he had experienced. He made excellent progress in treatment. After starting treatment, he became a citizen of the United States, opened his own restaurant, and sponsored numerous other Southeast Asian refugees as they came to the United States. At termination from his treatment, the social worker gave Mr. I the following poem (Lantz and Harper, 1991; Wimsatt, 1955). It reflects how Mr. I transformed the tragedies in his life and discovered a sense of meaning and purpose.

> He comes from Cambodia
>   and works sixteen hours a day
> seven days a week.
>   every week
> in his oriental restaurant
>   that pays his bills
> and lets him save enough
>   to bring another here
> from the camp he came through
>   after escaping the holocaust and the Khmer Rouge.
> Each one he brings is a holy prayer
>   for dead relatives
> and ancient ancestors
>   he has to leave behind.

The Curative Factors and Mr. I

At the start of social work treatment Mr. I had no hope that treatment might help. His previous treatment experience had confirmed his belief that his worldview could not be understood by a white social work practitioner. Mr. I believed that the mental health workers (both the first and the second) were not capable of relating to his guilt about his family and experiences in leaving Cambodia. Mr. I was surprised that the second social work practitioner understood his guilt. The worker's acceptance of his worldview allowed Mr. I to experience cleansing and hope, and to feel worthy of the help received from the different agencies in his social network. Mr. I was most pleased that he could find a way to give to the world in honor of his dead family members and the country he had to leave behind.

Conclusion

Asian Americans have been difficult to engage in social work practice because they have generally tried to maintain their social structure and culture with a minimum of visible conflict with the host society (Ho, 1976). Asians have tended to accept racism, discrimination, and prejudice from the dominant culture without voicing great protest (Ho, 1976; Lee and Saul, 1987). This process, as well as dominant culture stereotyping, has led to the dominant culture belief that Asian Americans are immune to the effects of white discrimination. The "quiet response" that Asian Americans have often given to discrimination is used by the dominant cultural group to minimize the need to provide services to the Asian American client (Ho, 1976). Social work intervention or other forms of social services are not easily accepted by Asian Americans as their heritage and diversity call for self-reliance, modesty, and dignity. Allowing outsiders, even professionals, to intervene in personal concerns continues to be an uncomfortable experience in view of usual cultural practices (Congress and Lyons, 1992).

The social work profession is accused of "underattention" to ethnic minorities, particularly Asians (Kim, 1995, p. 71). The dominant culture social work practitioner may have problems accepting that Asian clients sometimes express emotional and psychosocial problems through somatic complaints (Lee and Saul, 1987). Some modern social workers may become upset about some of the traditional views that many Asians accept about marital and family life (Ho, 1976) and will fail to develop empathy for the Asian client because of lack of understanding and even irritation about these Asian views (Ho, 1976; Lee, 1976; Lee and Saul, 1987). Many social work practitioners have difficulty working with Asian clients because they fail to understand that, for an Asian, admitting to an emotional problem may be a "loss of face" (Lee and Saul, 1987). The extent of family structure, self-control, and avoidance of shame is culturally unique to the Asian culture and poorly understood by most social workers. A western-world social worker does not interpret "shame" as being associated with not fulfilling social responsibilities. On the other hand, the eastern culture does not relate a sense of "shame" to failure and to self in debasing terms quite the same as do many other cultures, including America. These fundamental differences call for culturally sensitive social work practice to transcend the "melting-pot myth," particularly for Asian populations (Kim, 1995).

Lee and Saul (1987) report that the fundamental treatment skills needed to work with Asian clients are effective listening, empathy, accepting the client's worldview and view of distress, developing treatment goals that take into account the client's level of acculturation, understanding the Asian client's environmental situation, and understanding the level of discrimination and racism that Asian Americans experience in the United States today. Kim (1995) calls for professional recognition of the importance of reaching out to Asians who have historically not received social services. The importance of becoming culturally competent cannot be overstressed as only through increased knowledge and cross-cultural networks can a majority-culture social worker enter into the meaning world of a minority-culture client.

CHAPTER SIX

Migrating Clients

Many minority clients are also migrating clients. Such clients often experience considerable pain, frustration, and anomic depression in reaction to the migration process (Coles, 1968; Lantz and Harper, 1990). Anomie and anomic depression have often been described as forms of depression that occur in reaction to a sense of perceived meaninglessness (Frankl, 1959; Jilek, 1982; Krill, 1969). This sense of meaninglessness is sometimes called an "existential" or "meaning" vacuum (Frankl, 1988; Lantz, 1993). This existential vacuum, as described by Frankl (1959), has been measured as a separate clinical entity by Crumbaugh and Maholick (1966) through the use of their *Purpose in Life Test,* and by Elizabeth Lukas (1981) using her *Logotest.* The clinical entity has been observed in clinical practice by Frankl (1959), Jilek (1982), Krill (1969), Lukas (1981), Andrews (1974), Lantz (1978), Lantz and Harper (1989), Lifton (1973), and Coles.

An existential vacuum generally occurs in reaction to a disruption in the person's ability to experience a sense of meaning in life and is often characterized by feelings of emptiness and defeat, lowered self-esteem, discouragement, and, at times, moral disorientation (Frankl, 1959; Jilek, 1982; Lantz, 1978; Lantz and Harper, 1990). Such a condition occurs most frequently in times of cultural confusion or sociocultural disintegration or in periods of rapid change. This existential vacuum is common among persons who migrate to a new geographical area where a different and dominant cultural group disrupts a person's traditional methods of discovering and experiencing meaning (Lantz and Harper, 1990; Jilek, 1982; Harper and Lantz, 1992). For example, there often is an increased incidence of anomic depression and existential frustration among rural Appalachian people when they move to an urban setting in hope of finding employment and economic security (Lantz and Harper, 1989). In this situation the person may gain economic security, but lose traditional methods of discovering, symbolizing, and experiencing meaning that were used "back home" through the person's connection with nature, kin, and the extended family network (Lantz and Harper, 1989, 1990; Lantz, 1978; Coles, 1968).

It is not for existential frustration and meaning disruption to be simply viewed as "stress" and "problems of adjustment" (Locke, 1992; Fitzpatrick, 1987; Cravens and Bornemann, 1990; Moore and Pachon, 1985). For example, there has been great stress experienced in response to relocation among populations such as Puerto Ricans, Vietnamese, and Mexican Americans. Adjustment and assimilation demands following cross-cultural relocation are major stressors for migrating populations. Puerto Ricans have suffered discrimination and devaluation even though they hold citizenship. Cultural conflicts, particularly around values related to the centrality of extended family members and community bonds produce serious stress and disrupt meaning in life (Banks, 1987). Vietnamese have experienced great stress in their cross-cultural resettlement. Having fled their country and encountering hatred upon migration, Vietnamese have experienced serious loss and depression. For many relocated Vietnamese there have been great adjustment problems in a culture where language, religion, and racial prejudice are very different from that of their ethnic experience (Montero, 1979; Chan, 1986). Acculturation varies greatly among Mexican Americans who continue to flow into the southwestern United States, thus keeping alive strong ethnic ties to those recently left behind. Despite the stress associated with discrimination and exploitation, many seek upper-mobility and acculturation even in the presence of great emotional strain (Locke, 1992; Mirande, 1985; Burgos-Ocasio, 1996).

Cross-cultural relocation produces stress in response to changes in fundamental social supports and processes of one's ethnic background. Wagner (1993, 124) proposes that stress is culturally relative and that "understanding ethnic differences" is essential to understanding individual responses to stressors encountered upon migration. Different ethnic minority groups evidence varying responses to changes in daily practices and normative behaviors in experiences of cross-cultural relocation. Such responses include somatic distress, emotional distress, suicide, and deep depression. This commonly held view of stress recognizes the pain and distress that are experienced in many situations of cross-cultural relocation but does not address the great vulnerability for meaning disruption and loss of potential to discover meaning suffered by many who encounter new standards and normative behaviors in a different cultural context.

Although an existential vacuum is a frequent occurrence during times of migration, it can also occur in other situations that disrupt the person's ability to discover, experience, and perceive a sense of meaning and purpose in life (Lantz, 1978, 1986; Lantz and Harper, 1990). Any situation that disrupts meaning awareness is fertile soil for the occurrence of an anomic-existential vacuum (Frankl, 1959; Jilek, 1982; Lantz, 1987). The following four clinical illustrations are typical examples of an existential vacuum manifested by people who are migrating to a new place and a new life.

The M Family

The M family moved to the Midwest from Japan so Mr. M could continue employment with a Japanese manufacturing company that was opening an assembly plant. He was one of a group of Japanese managers chosen to plan and open the new plant. Mr. M spoke English, but his wife and three children spoke only Japanese. Approximately three months after her arrival in the United States, Mrs. M twisted and dislocated her eldest son's shoulder and then attempted suicide. Fortunately, her suicide attempt failed and she was admitted to a psychiatric hospital. In her initial treatment sessions, she reported to the translator and treatment staff that she felt empty and alone and that her life had seemed meaningless since she had come to America. She reported that her husband worked 12 hours a day and she was alone in a strange new country without friends, extended family, or support. She had not discovered a place to worship in her traditional manner and did not understand American ways. She said she had attempted to end her life because she felt useless and without hope. Mr. M reported that Mrs. M had never exhibited symptoms of depression in the past and had never before hurt the children.

The N Family

Mr. and Mrs. N came to the mental health center because Mrs. N was upset and depressed and had been "picking on" their two young children. Upon questioning, this "picking on" was more clearly described as "hitting and slapping." The N family had originally moved from Puerto Rico to New York City and then moved to the Midwest. Mrs. N reported that her children had been "getting on her nerves" since the move to the Midwest. Mr. N reported that his wife had never before hit the children. Mrs. N stated that she could find no Spanish people in the new city and that she wanted to return to New York. She felt uncomfortable at church as it was an Irish and Italian Catholic church, not a Spanish church. Mrs. N reported that at times she had received help in New York from a spiritualist, but she could not find one in the new city. She reported feeling empty, as if her life were meaningless.

The O Family

Mr. O was brought to a mental health center emergency unit by the police after they had responded to a domestic dispute request for help. He was intoxicated and had hit his wife with his fist. Mrs. O reported that Mr. O had never hit her or any other family member in the past. She said he had been drinking heavily, beginning about three months after the family had moved to the city from the mountains of eastern Tennessee. The family had moved to the Midwest because Mr. O's older sister had found him a factory job in the new city.

After sobering, Mr. O expressed considerable shame and guilt about his behavior. He reported that he had been feeling empty since he had moved to the city. He said he felt strange and had problems making friends with the people at his new job. He couldn't find a church where he felt comfortable and missed hunting, fishing, and roaming the woods as he had done "back home."

He reported that in spite of his new job and economic security, he felt hollow and empty.

The P Family

Mrs. P came to the mental health center because she felt depressed. She reported that she was experiencing crying spells and that her food tasted like cardboard. She was having problems sleeping and had lost 10 pounds since she had moved to the city from her home town. She and her husband had moved to a big city from their small, agricultural community because her husband, John, had a good job offer and a chance to go to college. The couple had a nine-month-old daughter, and Mrs. P stated that she was afraid she was not doing a good job as a mother since she had moved to the city. She said she was not neglecting her baby yet, but was afraid she might do so. At times, she had to push herself to feed and clothe the child. She reported that back home her mother and older sister had given her lots of reassurance and support and that she had lost them and all her favorite activities by moving. She now felt very alone. She felt empty and as if life were not as meaningful as it had been back home. She wanted help so she could feel better and have more energy.

Meaning and Migration Depression

The migration-meaning vacuum is described by the clients in these four clinical illustrations as a sense of emptiness and an inability to experience life as meaningful after migrating to a new geographical location. In each instance of meaning disruption, the client was separated from her or his usual methods for symbolizing and experiencing meaning.

For some migrating clients, the meaning vacuum is triggered by the client's separation from traditional methods of religious worship. The migrating-meaning vacuum may result from client's loss of contact with extended family, friends, kin, and clan. At times such a meaning vacuum is triggered by language difficulties that occur when a migrating person moves into a new culture. For other clients, a meaning vacuum is experienced in response to separation from familiar recreational and relaxation activities, such as walking in the hills "back home" (Lantz and Harper, 1989, 1990).

A migration-meaning vacuum is often a reactive, "crisis" problem, rather than a manifestation of a characterological or long-term personality problem (Lantz and Harper, 1989, 1990). Although a migration-meaning vacuum can be a manifestation of a narcissistic or borderline problem (Lantz, 1978, 1990), it is often a type of existential crisis triggered by a contextual event disrupting client meaning awareness. A reactive migration-meaning vacuum is a problem clients can often overcome when they are helped to rediscover a sense of purpose and meaning in life in their new location and new contextual situation (Lantz, 1991, 1993). The problem generally responds well to existential methods of intervention that make an active attempt to help the family reestablish a sense of meaning and purpose in life (Lantz and Harper, 1990; Lantz and Lantz, 1991). The following case illustration demonstrates many of the cross-cultural curative factors and how they can be used with a family that is experiencing a migration-meaning vacuum.

The Q Family

Mr. Q was brought to a hospital's emergency services unit by his cousin after overdosing on sleeping pills. Mr. Q said he had tried to kill himself because he felt guilty for hurting his baby. Mr. Q reported that he had lost his temper and spanked his two-year-old so hard it left bruises. He said that he left home so he would not do it again. After six days away from home, he went to a motel and overdosed on sleeping pills. He reported that he woke up a day later and called his cousin who talked him into getting help at the hospital.

Mr. Q reported that he had been feeling depressed for about four months. He said he had started feeling bad after he moved himself and his family to the city from his family home in West Virginia. He said he had never experienced such feelings previously. He had moved to the city for financial reasons after his cousin found him a factory job, but he began to have problems because he missed being back home. Mr. Q felt trapped because "there is no future back home" and because "I hate the city where there is a future." He said he wanted help, wanted to get back with his wife and children, and wanted to "find a way to stay in the city without getting crazy." He stated that he would not go back to his family until he was certain he could control his temper. He reported that he no longer wanted to kill himself. The following description of treatment gives an overview of the kind of help that was used to treat the Q family and illustrates the kind of social work practice that is often helpful in practice situations of a migration-meaning vacuum. Names, dates, and some of the circumstances of the practice situation have been changed to maintain confidentiality.

Mr. Q was initially seen in the emergency services unit of a general hospital early in 1983. He was first medically cleared by the hospital medical consultant, a specialist in internal medicine, then interviewed by a social worker. The social worker initially interviewed both Mr. Q and his cousin and later in the day conducted a family interview with both Mr. and Mrs. Q, their 16-year-old daughter, and two-year-old son. A caseworker from the local child protective agency also attended the last part of the social work interview. Based upon her assessment that the child abuse was a reaction to migration, the caseworker decided not to open a formal case so long as the Q family received outpatient services at the hospital. The caseworker and the Q family agreed that the caseworker would visit from time to time to see whether the family was benefitting from treatment and that no further incidents of abuse had occurred. Mrs. Q, the cousin, and the daughter all confirmed Mr. Q's report that he had had no problems with drinking or depression prior to moving to the city and that he had never hit anyone in his family in the past.

Mr. and Mrs. Q and the daughter were all given the Crumbaugh and Maholick *Purpose in Life Test* (1966) at the first family interview. Mr. Q scored 76, Mrs. Q 94, and the daughter 96. A score of less than 92 is a good indication that the subject is experiencing an existential vacuum. A score of 112 to 140 indicates that the subject is experiencing a sense of meaning and purpose in life, and a score of 92 to 111 indicates that the subject is vulnerable to the occurrence of an existential vacuum. The family *Purpose in*

Life Test score of 88.7, the mean score of the three tests given at the first interview, indicates that the Q family was, indeed, experiencing a family existential vacuum.

Based on family history, the *Purpose in Life Test* scores, and the social worker's observation of family interaction during the conjoint family interview, the social worker and consulting psychiatrist agreed that the Q family was suffering with a meaning vacuum triggered by family migration. The consulting psychiatrist agreed with the social worker that the family problems were reactive in nature and not the result of characterological problems. The psychiatrist did not feel that anyone in the family could benefit much from antidepressant medication and agreed with the social worker's plan to treat the Q family on an outpatient basis to help the family reestablish a sense of meaning in their new home in a new city.

The Q family remained in treatment for approximately one year. Slowly but surely, they learned to adjust to their new geographical and cultural situation and to integrate traditional family values, ideals, and behaviors into their current social and contextual situation. The Q family members have become active at a settlement house and also at their new church. At the present time, the Q family is very active, serving the function of "coach" at the settlement house, helping other migrant families of Appalachian heritage adjust to life and culture in an urban environment. At termination the family mean PIL score was 126. At the one-year follow up, the family mean PIL score was 124, and the family mean PIL score at the two-year follow up was 125. The family has not needed additional service.

Cross-Cultural Curative Factors in the Q Family

The Q family reported at the end of treatment that the social worker's help in linking them with resources (control) and in helping them talk with each other in a more effective manner (control) was extremely helpful. The family members reported that the social worker's questions helped them remember "what we stand for" (existential realization) and "what we are living for" (existential realization). The father reported that his relationship with the worker helped him regain his self-respect (cleansing). Mrs. Q felt that the worker tried hard to understand them and treat them with pride (worldview respect).

Conclusion

An existential vacuum frequently occurs during a period of migration that disrupts the minority culture client's traditional methods of discovering and experiencing meaning. In this chapter the authors have described the process of such a migration-meaning vacuum and offered a cross-cultural social work practice orientation to the treatment of this kind of human problem.

CHAPTER SEVEN

Appalachian Clients

Drawing national attention to impoverished families that filled every hollow and valley along the Appalachian region, the political agenda of the Kennedy administration gathered speed in its campaign against povery. This politically constructed region of the United States had the most severe poverty of the 1960s. The Appalachian region experienced a low standard of living, migration from the area, and social and economic problems that threatened the survival of those who lived there (Ergood and Kuhre, 1983; Obermiller and Olendick, 1986). An Appalachian client can be defined as a client who lives in or has migrated from one of the 397 counties defined as "Appalachia" by the federal government (Harper and Lantz, 1992; Lantz and Harper, 1989). The hills and valleys of the Appalachian mountain range offer rugged beauty and capture the love and lives of many who live there. Not all who are born in the region stay. Many Appalachian people leave their homes in search of employment where the same job or profession pays more in urban areas. Unemployed, often young, and with varying levels of education, many leave Appalachia to escape rural poverty and find financial security and economic opportunity in urban areas close to the region's boundaries (Harper and Lantz, 1992; Lantz and Harper, 1990).

With no respect for the lives of the Appalachian people, rural Appalachian poverty has developed primarily due to a lengthy period of land and resource control by large absentee financial and industrial corporations (Lantz and Harper, 1989). Appalachian history shows that the Appalachian people have experienced a series of disasters and exploitations, from the pillage of Appalachian forests by outsiders in the 1800s, to strip mining in the 1950s and 1960s, to the fall of oil prices and the resulting unemployment during the 1980s. The pillage of the Appalachian land by outside financial interests has left the Appalachian region bruised, broken, and traumatized (Lantz and Harper, 1989, 1990). It is not surprising that many Appalachian people have left their rural ancestral homes in search of economic opportunities and a higher standard of living (Lantz and Harper, 1989, 1990; Harper and Lantz, 1992).

The Appalachian Region

Appalachia lies along the Appalachian mountains, which extend from Georgia to New York, and includes four subregions. The northern section of Appalachia extends from New York into West Virginia and Ohio. This section of Appalachia has its economic base in steel, coal, and railroad transportation. A great reduction in employment has occurred in this region due to changing fuel consumption practices that have reduced the high production of coal (Appalachian Regional Commission, 1985; Lantz and Harper, 1989).

The highlands area of Appalachia includes parts of Pennsylvania and Maryland and reaches as far south as South Carolina and Georgia. From this subregion has come much of the mountaineer stereotype in which Appalachians are considered to be ignorant, primitive, and without normal values and goals (Lantz and Harper, 1989).

The third subregion of Appalachia is the central region which includes sixty contiguous counties in Virginia, West Virginia, Kentucky, and Tennessee. This section of Appalachia has had a history of the most grinding poverty in America (Lantz and Harper, 1989).

The southern region of Appalachia extends from Virginia through the Carolinas and into Alabama. This area is often considered to be dominated by the Ozark subculture but includes many unique regional folklore traditions (Campbell, 1983; Lantz and Harper, 1989).

Traditional Appalachian Identity

Understanding and appreciating the history of Appalachia are lenses for viewing human needs and shaping helpful intervention.

Regional folklore survives as tales of the life and times of mountain families are shared with younger generations. Played on stringed and often handmade instruments, homespun musical verse tells of love, pain, loss, and human endeavors. Arts and crafts highlight the region's beauty. Shelves of local bookstores and libraries document the previous struggles of economic ventures in natural resource industries through poetry, stories, and biographies. The region's subculture has a character similar to a patchwork showing the human endeavor of those who have lived in the region.

Some Appalachian families continue to reside on the farms and hills and in the communities of their ancestors. No other large geographic region in the United States has so many family members who live their lives in proximity to their birthplaces. Extended kinship networks offer protection from the outside world—from the severe poverty and bleak socioeconomic conditions in Appalachia (Greenlee and Lantz, 1992; Lantz and Harper, 1989). Newborn children are anxiously awaited and warmly welcomed into the "clan" and extended family network. In traditional Appalachian families, the individual learns from parents and clan. In this region, a family surname can identify persons and link them to a kinship network sometimes large enough to dominate a given hollow, mountain, or community (Lantz and Harper, 1989; Harper, 1974, 1981, 1983).

The phenomenon of clan surnames was an important variable in recent research by Keefe, Reck, and Reck (1991). Exploring educational experiences of lower-class southern Appalachian children compared to middle-class counterparts and relocated non-Appalachian children attending the schools, the study showed a strong association between social class and educational success. Regional surnames often identified children as being from lower-class families known in the region and consequently these children were targeted for discrimination and mistreatment by others in the school and community. The children's poverty directly correlated with their acceptance in the school system. Middle-class Appalachian school children suffered identity problems from stereotyping as "Appalachian," "redneck," or other labels. It was learned that middle-class children often resolved their identity confusion through education and out-migration, resulting in a loss of their cultural roots and heritage.

The study concluded that "rural, lower-class Appalachians are most distinctive in structural, cultural, and symbolic ways" (Keefe, Reck, and Reck, 1991). The study found that kinship systems in Appalachia form differently for traditional families and are particularly important for poor and lower-class families. These systems provide great support, mostly exclude nonrelatives, and are distinctive in having few exchanges with non-Appalachians (Rylant, 1982).

Somewhat mediated by social class and world experiences, families living in the Appalachian region are affected by regional ethnic values and practices and often struggle with their identity in response to the culture. Traditional Appalachian values and practices have long been handed down through intergenerational processes and include values such as independent self-reliance, stoicism, respect for elders, modesty, and a respect for tradition (Lantz and Harper, 1989; Batteau, 1983). These values can generally be grouped according to sense of religion and nature, sense of self, and sense of family and community.

Values of Traditional
Appalachian Clients

When an Appalachian moves from rural Appalachia to the city, they do not leave their Appalachian values "back home" (Lantz and Harper, 1989). Appalachian values are maintained in the city and, unfortunately, are often viewed as stumbling blocks to service provision by many middle-class social work practitioners who work in the service centers and agencies frequented by the urban poor (Obermiller and Maloney, 1991; Harper and Lantz, 1992; Harper and Greenlee, 1989, 1991). Appalachian value systems are frequently misunderstood by middle-class, non-Appalachian social workers. In order for social workers to be helpful to Appalachian families living in rural or urban settings and holding traditional Appalachian values, it is critically important that these values be understood. Traditional values include a present orientation with fatalistic views of the future, action versus dialogue, and fierce protection of self and kin (Harper, 1996). Personal values of traditional Appalachians are of great importance and fall into three major categories: sense of self, sense of religion and nature, and sense of family and community (Jones, L., 1983; Harper and Lantz, 1992; Harper, 1996).

Sense of Religion and Nature

Appalachian people demonstrate a deep sense of appreciation for nature and natural beauty and link their sense of connection with the world around them to religious meaning. They are religious in that the meanings they see in life primarily come from religious sources and from creation (Jones, L., 1983). In order to more fully understand Appalachian religious values, it is important to understand the history of religion in Appalachia.

When immigrants came to live in the Appalachian mountains, they were Presbyterians, Episcopalians, and members of the other mainline religious denominations mostly from England, Scotland, Wales, Holland, Germany, and Ireland (Jones, L., 1983). Such mainline denomination churches generally required a centralized organization that was very impractical in the Appalachian wilderness. The people of the Appalachian mountains were basically abandoned in the early years by the central administrations of the major denominations, resulting in local and autonomous sects in the Appalachian region. These individualistic churches stressed the fundamentals of religious faith and depended only on local resources for leadership and development.

Life on the Appalachian mountain frontier was extremely hard and did not encourage the development of an optimistic social gospel in the independent Appalachian churches. In Appalachia, hard work did not bring a sure reward, and so Appalachian religion often became extremely fatalistic and stressed rewards in another life. The important purpose in such a religion is to reap rewards in eternity, which in the Appalachian tradition means to "accept Jesus as one's personal savior" (Jones, L., 1983, p. 125). This fatalistic religion was and still is a realistic religion that fits a realistic people who have endured a life history of poverty and hardship (Harper, 1996). Many of the Appalachian values discussed in this chapter have religious origins.

Seeking meaning through religion and through nature, Appalachian people seem to fall deeply in love with their native birthplace and the place of their childhood. Appalachian people seem to always "think of going back for good" (Jones, L., 1983, p. 127). The Appalachian's love of place has much to do with the kinship network and the natural rural or mountainous beauty of the Appalachian person's special place in family and region. Many Appalachian people who migrate to urban areas express feelings of discomfort and loss attached to living in concrete cities where the beauty of nature cannot be seen and where they feel greater distance from God and nature (Obermiller and Maloney, 1991; Lantz and Harper, 1989; Harper, 1992).

The Appalachian individual's love of beauty includes a reverence for nature and a religious belief that beauty in the world is a reflection of God's love (Lantz and Harper, 1989). Appalachian people have a strong sense of beauty and have developed many art forms which are often called folk art by people who do not come from an Appalachian heritage. In Appalachia, there has always been great pride in good craftsmanship, and much time is spent to make a useful household item more attractive (Jones, L., 1983).

Sense of Self

Self-reliance, pride, and individualism are three fairly accurate characteristics of the Appalachian people. The forebears of the Appalachian people came to the region to escape encroachments on freedoms in their native countries such as England, Ireland, Germany, Scotland, and Wales. Coming to a new country and living in the wilderness reinforced the need for self-reliance. In the Appalachian wilderness, one could not survive without a high degree of self-reliance and individualism. Not inconsistent with self-reliance, many Appalachians are well informed about their well-being and survival in terms of health and nutrition, areas where great care and modern health practices are often evidenced (Harper, 1996).

The pride of the Appalachian people comes from the tradition of self-reliance. Appalachian people have a strong sense of self and a feeling of not wanting to be indebted to other people. Appalachian people find it hard to seek resources in the face of poverty such as welfare aid and community medical treatment (Greenlee and Lantz, 1993). The value of self-reliance among Appalachian people is often stronger than the desire to get help (Jones, L., 1983, p. 126).

A major goal for most Appalachian people is to relate well with other people. Appalachian people will go to great lengths to keep from offending anyone. In Appalachia, it is often more important to get along and have a good relationship with other people than it is to make one's true feelings understood (Jones, L., 1983, p. 126; Lantz and Harper, 1989).

Since the Appalachian person wants to "get along," the Appalachian individual is often very willing to respect other people and their differences. Loyal Jones reports that most Appalachians believe that "every man ought to have the right to make a fool out of himself." Appalachian people tend to accept people on a personal basis and to not judge people on how they look, their race, gender, credentials, or accomplishments (Jones, L., 1983, p. 127).

Appalachian people feel that it is wrong to brag, to put on airs, to "not boast nor try to get above our raising" (Jones, L., 1983, p. 127). Appalachian people do not generally talk about their virtues. In Appalachia, there is not a great deal of reinforced competition, and people who are especially skilled in a particular endeavor are often reluctant to perform in order to protect the feelings of those who are less skilled. Appalachian people are humble, mostly realistic in their view of themselves, and find it offensive to pretend to be something other than what they are. Quick to laugh at their own behaviors, there are wit, laughter, and regional stories and jokes that bring joy to many conversations. Appalachian people have a good sense of humor and believe that humor is a gift of God that sustains people in hard times (Greenlee and Lantz, 1993). Appalachians are very comfortable laughing at their own behaviors and such humor is often tied up in their religious understanding of concepts of humankind. Appalachians use humor to fight a human tendency towards pride and also use it to highlight "pretensions to power and perfection" (Jones, L., 1983, p. 128). Appalachians feel free to poke a great deal of fun at pompous people and often like to develop interesting sayings about them. A good example of such humorous sayings is reported by Loyal Jones who reports that "preachers and lawyers and buzzard eggs—there's more hatched than ever comes to perfection" (Jones, L., 1983, p. 128).

Sense of Family and Community

The Appalachian person's focus upon pride and independence is softened a bit by a basic sense of hospitality and neighborliness (Jones, L., 1983). On the Appalachian frontier, it was necessary for neighbors to help each other build homes and barns and to care for each other in times of sickness and bad health. As a result, the tradition of helping a neighbor exists even in urban Appalachian ghetto neighborhoods where people stick together to fight poverty, hunger, and economic deprivation (Lantz and Harper, 1989, 1990; Obermiller and Maloney, 1991).

Appalachian people share strong kinship values centered in family tradition. The Appalachian person feels most clearly a desire to please his or her family and feels most comfortable when in the family circle. Family loyalty runs deep between family members in the Appalachian family where a sense of responsibility for each other often extends to cousins, nephews, nieces, uncles, aunts, and even in-laws (Jones, L., 1983; Greenlee and Lantz, 1992). Familial blood ties are very strong in Appalachia. Family therapy is often considered a very reasonable idea by the Appalachian client, as family treatment fits well with the love of family which runs deep in the Appalachian tradition and system of values (Lantz and Harper, 1989, 1990; Harper and Lantz, 1992).

The importance of family and community supports a strong sense of patriotism. Appalachian people are extremely patriotic and see it as a duty to serve in the armed forces of our country. This love of country is reactive to the Appalachian's love of a country that they perceive gives people the freedom to be themselves and provides the opportunity to be independent and to worship God in an independent way. It is a much noted fact that draft quotas in Appalachia have often been filled by volunteers throughout our country's history. When visiting an Appalachian family in their home, it is not unusual to see photographs of family members in uniform who have died in service to their country. Many liberal social workers who have a personal antiwar philosophy "turn off" Appalachian clients by making statements that seem unpatriotic to Appalachian people and which seem disrespectful to their kin who have died in war (Lantz, 1974).

Appalachian Out-Migration and the Search for Security

It is estimated that eventually seven million people migrated from Appalachia between 1940 and 1990 (Obermiller and Olendick, 1986; Ergood and Kuhre, 1991). Most Appalachian migrants have moved toward industrial centers, particularly the auto assembly factories in Michigan and in Ohio. Since 1980, the speed of Appalachian migration has decreased and the direction of most migration has changed from the north to the southwest regions of the country (Lantz and Harper, 1989).

When Appalachian people move to the city, they often discover that they have exchanged rural poverty and unemployment for urban poverty and unemployment (Obermiller and Maloney, 1991; Lantz and Harper, 1989, 1990; Harper and Lantz, 1992). This flight from rural poverty to urban poverty often creates a disruption in meaning awareness for the migrating Appalachian. Such a disruption in meaning awareness is reactive to poverty, migration, and the Appalachian person's loss of a supporting kinship network. This disruption of meaning awareness and sense of anomie are often followed with a variety of problems and emotional symptoms that the Appalachian client often labels and calls "nerves" (Lantz, 1992; Lantz and Harper, 1989, 1990; Harper and Lantz, 1992).

Developing and providing social work services for Appalachian people requires that the social work provider have specific knowledge of the very special needs of this traditional and often fundamentalist group (Lantz and Harper, 1989). The social worker should gain an understanding of the values, beliefs, and lifestyles of clients who live or have lived within the Appalachian region (Keefe, 1988; Harper, 1996). Developing an empathic and caring approach to social work practice with this Appalachian client requires a basic understanding of the ethos of the region and its socioeconomic problems (Harper, 1986; Lantz and Harper, 1989). The continuing pattern of Appalachian migration for the purpose of finding work and economic security has resulted in Appalachian-urban neighborhoods in sections of cities throughout Ohio and also in Chicago, Detroit, Pittsburgh, and Gary, Indiana. Often such neighborhoods become crowded low-income ghettoes where Appalachian poverty, inability to access urban resources, and a different orientation to person and place challenge urban human service, education, and medical professionals (Lantz and Harper, 1989, 1990; Harper and Lantz, 1992).

Disruption of Social Functioning in Response to Migration

The flight of Appalachian people from rural poverty to urban poverty has often disrupted self-esteem, a sense of meaning and purpose in life, and general social functioning for the migrating Appalachian family or individual (Lantz and Harper, 1989, 1990). Even when an Appalachian person does find a job in the city, the person will still often lose the sense of kinship, place, and beauty experienced back home. If the person is unable to find a job, the losses in moving to the city are compounded by being no better off financially. Instead, many migrants trade rural poverty for urban poverty (Lantz and Harper, 1989). The Appalachian person and the Appalachian family are frequently caught in a socioeconomic double bind. If the Appalachian does not move to the city, there is very little hope of a good economic future. If the Appalachian person does move to the city, they may receive a little more economic hope, but only in exchange for a loss of support, beauty, and the kinship system which existed back home.

Appalachian individuals and families who do move to the city are seldom welcomed with "open arms" by city officials, police, educators, and human service professionals (Lantz and Harper, 1989). Both authors of this book have witnessed and been amazed that so many urban helping professionals view relocated Appalachian people as "backward, stupid, rednecks, bumpkins, and hillbillies." We have also been shocked at how easily child welfare workers, mental health workers, and educators have modeled extreme disrespect for Appalachian parents in front of their children, particularly in urban, Appalachian settlements. In our opinion, mainstream urban America does not seem to understand the respect which is deserved by ethical, respectful, hardworking Appalachian families and family members who have often endured grinding poverty and, yet, have the courage to enter an emotionally foreign urban territory in the hope of improving their economic circumstances.

Case Example—Relocated Appalachian Client

It is evident that living within the boundaries of a nation does not connote homogeneous lifestyle or expectations. One example of diversity within the American society is evidenced by lifestyles within Appalachia. Personal and human differences within the region give people a very different worldview. Providing opportunities for relocated clients to discover and experience meaning in their new sociocultural context is an important role for social workers. The following case illustration demonstrates some of the healing factors that we believe to be helpful in social work practice with the Appalachian client.

Mr. H

Mr. H was referred for social work treatment by his family doctor on the near west side of Columbus, Ohio. The family doctor believed that Mr. H was demonstrating emotional problems by overly focusing on minor physical problems and concerns. Mr. H believed that he was "suffering with nerves." His family doctor reported that Mr. H had been given and had kept 31 medical appointments in 1988 and that almost all of these appointments were not necessary from a medical standpoint. Mr. H was of Appalachian heritage and had moved to Columbus, Ohio, from West Virginia in search of economic and financial security. Mr. H reported that he had a decent factory job that paid well, that he had moved to Columbus two years ago, and that he hated being in the city "where I got a chance to make it financially." He said that he wanted to go back home to West Virginia, but realized that there was no job for him there. He had stopped going to church because he could not find one like the church back home. Mr. H reported that he stayed at his apartment most of the time and felt uncomfortable in the city so did not go out. He said that he missed a lot of work because of his "nerves" and had been drinking some to calm him. Mr. H scored a 79 on the Crumbaugh and Maholick (1966) *Purpose in Life Test* at his second social work appointment. A score of less than 92 is considered a good indication that the client is experiencing a disruption in his or her sense of meaning and purpose in life.

The goal of social work treatment with Mr. H was to help him either adjust more effectively to life in the city or to help him decide to move back to West Virginia if he so desired. Mr. H also needed to understand that his "nerves" were a result of his difficulty in experiencing a sense of meaning and purpose in life in the city and that in order to decrease his "nerves" he would have to rediscover the meanings, values, and meaning potentials that he could actualize and create in the city.

During the initial stage of social work treatment, Mr. H missed a number of scheduled social work appointments and did not seem motivated to engage in social work treatment. Mr. H reported that he wanted pills for his nerves and did not understand why his family doctor had referred him for counseling.

There was a remarkable change in Mr. H's attitude toward social work treatment and his willingness to work in treatment after his social worker had him read out loud George Ella Lyon's (1990) small children's book *Come a Tide* in the fifth social work interview. In this outstanding children's book, the central character is a young Appalachian woman who describes a flood and her family's problems resulting from the flood. In the story, the family home was flooded, and after the waters went back down, the family members discovered that the flood had buried the family treasures in mud, goo, and slime. In the story, the grandmother reported, "It's time to make friends with a shovel." The entire family started to work. The family members "dug and hauled and scrubbed and crawled" and were eventually able to find their "buried treasures."

After Mr. H read this story, the social worker asked him to explain its meaning and why he felt the social worker wanted him to read the story. Mr. H reported that he could now see that his move to the city had "flooded" his life and that "I better start digging to get it back." Mr. H reported that his frayed nerves made sense in that the "stuff that means something to me has been flooded out when I moved to the city." Mr. H decided that it was the social worker's job to "help me make friends with a shovel" and to "dig out a decent life in the city."

During social work with Mr. H, the worker provided him with many opportunities to ventilate and express sadness about the losses he had experienced by moving to the city (in other words, cleansing). The worker provided many existential reflection experiences to help Mr. H become more aware of the values and meanings he wanted to find and experience in the city. The worker also linked Mr. H to an Appalachian club at a city settlement house and to a fundamentalist church that was similar to Mr. H's church back home. The worker also showed Mr. H some good fishing spots near the city so that Mr. H could regain one of his favorite activities that he had loved. Mr. H came to twenty-three social work appointments over an eight-month period of treatment. At termination, Mr. H scored 123 on the *Purpose in Life Test,* his family doctor reported that he was no longer making unnecessary medical appointments, and Mr. H reported that he was feeling much better and no longer was drinking to help his nerves.

Curative Factors Used with Mr. H

In social work treatment with Mr. H, the worker did an outstanding job respecting Mr. H's worldview and using the flood story to help Mr. H include social work treatment in his worldview. Catharsis was an important aspect of treatment with Mr. H, as was the curative factor of control that resulted from the worker's linking and environmental modification activities. The previously mentioned activities provided Mr. H with a sense of hope. It was important for Mr. H that the worker encouraged him to replace his values both back home and in the city. Mr. H considered these existential realization and reflection experiences to be an important part of the help he received.

Summary

Appalachian clients suffer poverty, class discrimination, and prejudice against their traditional values and norms. Many Appalachian people have moved to the city to escape rural poverty only to find this rural poverty replaced by urban poverty. The Appalachian client's poverty, loss of a kinship network, and the supports from "back home" often combine to create and trigger many difficult human problems such as anxiety, depression, and a disruption of the sense of meaning and purpose in life.

CHAPTER EIGHT

Vietnam Veteran Clients

When Mr. V first started social work treatment he reported, "I felt like an immigrant from another country when I first came back from service in Vietnam." Like so many other veterans of the Vietnam War, Mr. V has been treated like a stranger in his own country. Soldiers and military personnel who served in the Vietnam War represented human diversity in terms of race, gender, ethnicity, religion, and worldview. In view of human diversity among veterans and the shared experience of war in a very culturally different setting, it can be extremely helpful to view social work practice with the Vietnam veteran as a cross-cultural helping process. Many Vietnam veterans experience the same kinds of anomic and existential difficulties as do the other minority culture or special population clients described in this book.

This approach to cross-cultural social work practice with Vietnam veterans is based upon a belief in the central, core importance of helping Vietnam veterans discover and experience a sense of meaning in both their Vietnam memories and their future lives (Lantz, 1974, 1978, 1989, 1991, 1993, 1994, 1995; Lantz and Greenlee, 1990). In this approach it is believed that a failure to discover such a sense of meaning results in what Frankl (1959) has called an existential-meaning vacuum and Krill (1969) has called the problem of anomie. If this vacuum is not filled by a developing sense of meaning and purpose in life, it will be filled instead by symptoms and problems such as some forms of anxiety, depression, sexual problems, substance abuse, episodic discontrol, emotional numbness, social withdrawal, or interpersonal isolation (Frankl, 1959; Lantz, 1990; O'Brien, 1969; Mason, 1985; Tick, 1989; Criswell, 1991). Some Vietnam veterans report flashback experiences and intrusive memories that often rush in to fill and signal the presence of an existential vacuum (Williams, 1983; Brende and Parson, 1985; Lantz, 1993; Lifton, 1973).

From a cross-cultural point of view, social work practice with the Vietnam veteran should be directed toward facilitating the veteran's personal search for meaning and purpose in life (Lantz and Greenlee, 1990). The treatment approach should be directed toward helping the Vietnam veteran overcome disruptions of his or her search for meaning (Lifton, 1973; Williams, 1983; Lantz, 1974, 1990). This shrinks the existential vacuum and limits the opportunity for symptom development (Frankl, 1959; Lantz and Pegram, 1989; Lantz and Greenlee, 1990).

Treacherous Terrain

The Vietnam War is considered to have officially started on August 5, 1964, and to have ended on May 7, 1975 (Williams, 1983). Approximately 4 million American men and women served their country in Southeast Asia with our armed forces during the Vietnam War (Brende and Parson, 1985; Lifton, 1973). Many of these veterans still suffer emotional pain caused by their exposure to the horrors of this war and to their country's failure to welcome them back home in a sincere and meaningful way (Brende and Parson; Williams, 1983; Tick, 1989; Lifton; Green, 1989). Alcohol and substance abuse are serious problems for some Vietnam veterans who use these chemicals in an attempt to numb the pain associated with flashback episodes and intrusive memories of the war (Lantz, 1989, 1990; Tick).

Some Vietnam veterans report that they have not had emotional problems in reaction to their experiences in Vietnam. Others report serious emotional responses and problems, such as terrifying flashback experiences, powerful intrusive memories, substance abuse, emotional withdrawal, and episodic discontrol (Lifton, 1973; Lantz, 1991; MacPherson, 1984). It is difficult to understand why some Vietnam veterans experience problems and others do not. Some authorities (Brende and Parson, 1985; MacPherson) have suggested that the intensity of the veteran's symptoms corresponds to the level of horror experienced in the war, the degree of moral conflict experienced in response to the war, and the degree of personal culpability gained from the experience of war. A simpler "existential" formula is probably more accurate and useful in the clinical practice situation. From an existential standpoint, the intensity of the Vietnam veteran's symptoms and problems is generally reactive to the amount of horror experienced or observed during the war and the degree of success the veteran has had in discovering a sense of meaning and purpose in his or her personal Vietnam experiences (Lantz, 1974, 1993; Lantz and Greenlee, 1990).

Neither the Vietnam veteran nor the social worker can change the amount of horror that the veteran experienced during the war. What can be changed is the veteran's ability to discover and experience a sense of meaning and purpose in her or his memories of the war. This kind of meaning recovery can provide considerable relief from emotional pain (Frankl, 1959; Lantz, 1987) and can offer the veteran dramatic treatment results (Lantz, 1978, 1991; Tick, 1989; Williams, 1983; Lantz and Greenlee, 1990).

The Vietnam Veteran and the Search for Meaning

A large proportion of American citizens believes that the United States should not have become involved in the Vietnam War (Tick, 1989; Green, 1989). Lindy (1988), Green (1989), Tick, and MacPherson (1984) have all dramatically documented the disrespect and even hatred that have been heaped upon many Vietnam veterans as they have returned home to the United States after facing the sheer challenge of physical survival and of watching many of their friends die in extremely violent ways. The important meaning potential of the societal ritual of welcoming our young soldiers back home was disrupted by our country's ambivalent feelings about the Vietnam War (Lantz, 1978, 1989; Mason, 1985). At times, the veterans who survived the war could not survive the message they received from their country. This message communicated the view that their acts of courage, suffering, and patriotism did not "mean anything" (Lifton, 1973; Lantz and Greenlee, 1990). Such a message seemed to come from the veterans' government, their communities, and, at times, from family and childhood friends (Green, 1989; O'Brien, 1969; Tick). The failure of society to say "thank you" frequently disrupted and limited the Vietnam veteran's search for meaning. This societal meaning disruption has made an existential approach to cross-cultural social work a particularly effective method of treatment to use with the Vietnam veteran. The following two clinical illustrations demonstrate the potential usefulness of this social work approach with many Vietnam veterans.

Mr. W

Mr. W and his wife requested social work treatment in 1981. He had lost a leg in Vietnam as a result of a mortar attack. The original presenting problem that was very upsetting to his wife was his emotional withdrawal. When Mr. W became upset, he would leave her and the children and be gone for days. Mr. W reported that his avoidance was used to "protect" his wife and his adolescent children. He reported that he did not want to explode emotionally while he was having intrusive thoughts and flashback experiences.

Although Mr. W believed his intrusive thoughts were bad and dangerous, the social worker attempted to help him see that they might also have an adaptive function (control). The social worker attempted to help Mr. W to understand that persons who experience traumatic events usually undergo a healing process and that part of this process is a search for meaning in the face of the trauma and tragedy. The social worker reported his belief that the intrusive thoughts and flashbacks might be Mr. W's unconscious way of attempting to discover, rediscover, and experience a sense of meaning that might be hidden in his painful memories and intrusive thoughts.

Mr. W was unwilling to talk about his memories on an outpatient basis, but did agree to go into a psychiatric hospital for a short period of time so that he could begin to talk about his memories with the social worker in the safe atmosphere of the hospital setting (control). He remained in the hospital for six weeks in 1981 and got a good start at openly "talking out" his memories with both the social worker in individual therapy and with his wife in marital therapy (cleansing). As Mr. W began to talk, he reported that he was beginning to develop a "feeling of meaning" about his Vietnam experiences (existential realization). He started to understand the social worker's point of view that painful, intrusive memories often are, as Williams (1983) pointed out, a signal of meaning repression.

From 1981 through 1987, the social worker worked with the couple in an attempt to help Mr. W continue to share his past and to rediscover meaning and purpose in his past. By the beginning of 1987, Mr. W had told his wife most of the stories from his experience. As he revealed his memories and developed a sense of meaning regarding his Vietnam past, he experienced a great reduction in flashbacks and intrusive thoughts. These memories diminished in both intensity and frequency. Mr. W eventually stopped feeling afraid that he might explode (control). In early 1987 he described everything as fine, except that his leg still hurt. He could not understand "how a leg you no longer have can still hurt like hell."

Toward the end of 1987, Mr. W asked the social worker whether the social worker would go to Washington, D.C., with him to "see the wall" (Vietnam War Memorial). The social worker had a strong sense that he should honor Mr. W's request even if it was not a technically correct thing to do (worldview respect). The trip was very emotional and powerful for both Mr. W and the social worker. The specific details are not as important as the fact that Mr. W stopped feeling pain in his absent leg once he experienced the memorial (cleansing). In some way the trip helped him to finally discover meaning in the loss of his leg (existential realization). He has suffered no more phantom pain since this trip.

Mr. X

Mr. X began his treatment relationship with a social worker in a residential facility for the treatment of substance abuse problems in 1984. He was a retired Army sergeant major who had served three tours in Vietnam. Mr. X had been admitted to the unit because of serious alcohol abuse. Upon admission, Mr. X did not believe that he was alcoholic, but did admit that "something was wrong." He had agreed to enter treatment only because his wife had threatened to leave him if he did not seek help. The precipitating factor that led to his admission was an incident where he had become extremely violent while intoxicated, threatened his wife and family, and physically destroyed the house trailer in which they lived.

Early in the program, Mr. X denied the existence of any major problems in his life, but both his daughter and wife spoke of being afraid of him. His wife reported that he would have recurrent nightmares of his Vietnam experiences but refused to talk with her about those experiences. He was quick to lose his temper and his family no longer trusted him. His alcohol consumption had increased, and for the first time in his life, he had received a citation for driving while intoxicated.

In the second week of treatment, the social worker began to explore the possibility that Mr. X was suffering from post-traumatic stress disorder syndrome (PTSD) in reaction to his experiences in Vietnam. The social worker confronted Mr. X in group therapy during the presentation of his autobiography. It was here that Mr. X chose to share with the group that he suffered from recurrent and intrusive recollections of an event in Vietnam where his best friend had been killed. Mr. X felt responsible for his friend's death. He talked about the loss of this closest friend and his feelings of guilt about having survived (cleansing).

Mr. X spoke with the group and his social worker about the tremendous shame he felt upon returning to the United States and being called a "baby killer." He stated that he had entered the war with a purpose—to defend democracy. He left Vietnam not understanding the purpose of the war, and he could no longer make sense of his involvement. His method of coping with this loss of meaning was to attempt to medicate his pain and guilt with alcohol.

The social worker's practice with Mr. X focused upon helping him to find meaning in the pain he had encountered in Vietnam (existential realization). Through his suffering and rediscovery of meaning, Mr. Y has learned the difference between survivor's guilt and survivor's responsibility. He is now committed to helping other Vietnam veterans who have drinking problems and is very active in the Vietnam veterans' self-help movement (control, cleansing, and existential realization). His intrusive thoughts and nightmares have greatly lessened in intensity and frequency. In addition, he no longer fears losing control of his temper (control), and he has reestablished an intimate and meaningful relationship with his wife and family. He no longer drinks.

Potential Vietnam Veteran Symptoms

Both Mr. W and Mr. X exhibited a number of problems and symptoms that are very common reactions of many veterans to experiences of the Vietnam War. At times these problems and symptoms present in a clinical cluster that is generally labeled post-traumatic stress disorder (Haley, 1974; Lantz, 1993; Williams, 1983; Lantz and Greenlee, 1990). The authors agree with Williams (1983), Lifton (1973), and Tick (1989), who recommend that the clinical symptom cluster be called a "response" instead of a disorder. In our opinion it would be abnormal for Vietnam veterans not to be upset about the way they were treated, both during and after the war. Some of the common problems found when a Vietnam veteran is suffering from post-traumatic stress response include anesthesia, rage, anxiety, depression, substance abuse, intrusive thoughts, and flashback experiences (Haley; Williams, 1983; Lantz, 1991; Lifton; Tick; Mason, 1985; O'Brien, 1969).

Anesthesia

Many Vietnam veterans suffering with PTSD appear cold, distant, detached, and uninvolved. Such an appearance generally results from the veteran's attempt to repress and suppress painful memories and feelings and to maintain a sense of personal control (Williams, 1983; Lifton, 1973; Lindy, 1988). Many Vietnam veterans report that they fear these feelings because "once they begin to come out, who knows what might happen?" (Tick, 1989). The Vietnam veteran's attempt to control and numb these feelings has the negative side effect of also disrupting meaning awareness. Through the process of suppressing feelings and painful memories, veterans also suppress opportunities to discover and experience meanings hidden in the painful feelings and memories of their Vietnam past (Lifton; Lantz, 1990, 1993; Lindy).

Rage

Many Vietnam veterans suffering with PTSD report that they experience intense feelings of anger and rage. Often such feelings are directed toward authority figures, such as politicians, helpers, and military officials. Many Vietnam veterans believe they have been treated with profound disrespect by their former commanding officers, by their country, and by their communities (Tick, 1989). Such feelings of rage sometimes serve as a screening device, in that if the helper or authority figure is not "run off" by the veteran's rage, there is a chance that the helper will be able to handle and accept the terror and horror embedded in the veteran's memories of the war (Lantz, 1974, 1990; Lindy, 1988; Lifton, 1973).

Anxiety

Many Vietnam veterans suffering with PTSD act in a hypervigilant way (Lantz, 1991). They often scan their environment and avoid crowded public areas. Both open and confined spaces can be a source of anxiety for many Vietnam veterans, who often prefer to keep their backs to a solid object, such as a corner or a wall. Such hypervigilant behaviors are often described as pathological by psychotherapists and social workers who have not served in a war zone situation. However, such behaviors often seem very understandable to a social worker who has personally experienced war (Lantz, 1974, 1993; Brende and Parson, 1985).

Depression

Depression is a very common symptom experienced by many Vietnam veterans suffering with PTSD. Classic manifestations of depression, such as psychomotor retardation, sleep disturbances, appetite disturbances, concentration problems, and suicidal ideation, are frequently experienced by Vietnam veterans. We believe that such symptoms of depression often rush in to fill an existential vacuum when veterans have not been able to discover and experience a sense of meaning in their Vietnam past (Lantz, 1993; Lifton, 1973; Lindy, 1988; Lantz and Greenlee, 1990).

Intrusive Thoughts and Flashback Experiences

Traumatic memories of Vietnam often intrude into the consciousness of the veteran, both at night and during the day (Lifton, 1973). At times such intrusive thoughts are connected with intrusive imagery. Such thoughts and imagery may trigger anxiety, frustration, sadness, or rage and are often themselves triggered by stimuli that remind veterans of their Vietnam past. Loud noises, blood, camouflage clothing (such as hunting shirts), airplane noises, helicopter noises, and even rainy weather may all be potent stimuli to trigger painful memories and intrusive imagery for the Vietnam veteran. We agree with Williams (1983) and Tick (1989), who suggest that such intrusive thoughts and imagery often contain opportunities to help veterans discover and experience a sense of meaning in their Vietnam past, and that the process of helping the veteran to "talk out" these memories can result in an enhanced level of meaning potential awareness. Such therapeutic existential reflection will not occur until the veteran trusts that the listener will not "run away" from his or her horrible memories and emotional pain (Haley, 1974; Lantz, 1990; Lindy, 1988; Lantz and Greenlee, 1990).

Substance Abuse

Some Vietnam veterans suffering with PTSD escape terrifying memories through the use of alcohol and drugs (Lindy, 1988; Lifton, 1973; Lantz, 1991). At times drugs and alcohol are used by the veteran to control the emptiness and pain that can fill the existential-meaning vacuum. Although substance abuse does help the Vietnam veteran to control pain initially, this self-medicating strategy also disrupts meaning awareness and promotes depression. The social worker who successfully helps the Vietnam veteran to stop abusing drugs and alcohol must be willing to empathically share the pain that will then emerge (Haley, 1974; Lifton; Lindy; Lantz and Greenlee, 1990).

A Final Case Illustration: Mrs. Y

Mrs. Y requested treatment in January, 1980, because she had started drinking heavily since her engagement. She had been an Army nurse stationed in Vietnam for 18 months from 1969 to 1970. At that time she was 22 years old. Working in emergency surgery in an Army surgical hospital, she had toiled extremely long hours to save the lives of severely wounded American soldiers. She reported that she had learned to tolerate the blood and gore by "building a wall and becoming numb."

Mrs. Y did not volunteer for a second tour of duty. She left the Army to return to civilian life and to work as a stepdown surgical nurse in a large Midwest hospital. In this job, she was expected once again to make life and death decisions and to function adequately in a crisis situation. She reported that her ability to "go numb and build a wall" again served her well.

Mrs. Y reported that she had lived an organized, systematic, lonely, and emotion-free life until she had met "Sam" in 1979. According to her, "Sam broke down my wall and I started to feel." Soon she started having flashback experiences where she again saw bloody and broken bodies just before falling asleep. She also started drinking to help her go to sleep.

In this clinical situation, a 22-year-old Vietnam veteran nurse exposed to the terrible gore and death associated with Vietnam combat wounds had learned to handle the terror of the situation by building a wall and going numb. This response protected her from the pain of her Vietnam experiences but also kept her from experiencing a sense of meaning and purpose in the valuable job she had done saving American lives during her time in Vietnam. When she fell in love, she was pushed to grieve "the young men I lost in Vietnam." Her relationship with Sam forced her to put down her wall and to reexperience both the pain and meaning she had originally repressed in Vietnam.

Social work practice with Mrs. Y focused upon facilitating her "recovery of meaning" (existential realization) through the process of existential reflection. Network intervention was also employed to connect her with other Vietnam veterans who could offer empathy and support (cleansing and control). During conjoint treatment sessions with both Mrs. and Mr. Y, the techniques of social skills training helped her learn to communicate with her husband in a more open and honest way (control). She terminated treatment in 1986, which was one year after the birth of her son and two years after her last flashback experience.

Conclusion

Cross-cultural social work with Vietnam veterans should be directed toward helping them discover a sense of meaning and purpose both in their future and in their Vietnam past. Such a developing sense of purpose and meaning shrinks those symptoms that grow in the existential-meaning vacuum. Existential realization, cleansing experiences, and control are three cross-cultural social work curative factors that are often especially helpful to Vietnam veterans in their personal search for meaning and purpose in life (Lantz, 1974, 1990, 1993; Lantz and Greenlee, 1990).

CHAPTER NINE

Traumatized Clients

The horror of violence touches the lives of many people in the United States of America. It is estimated that close to 50 percent of all people living in the United States have suffered the effects of violence (Figley, 1990; Lantz, 1974, 1978). Many of the population groups discussed in this book have suffered extreme violence and cruelty in reaction to prejudice, discrimination, and outright hatred (Lantz and Pegram, 1989, 1990; Lantz and Harper, 1990; Brende and Parson, 1985; Mwanza, 1990). For this reason the authors of this text believe it is important to include a chapter on treatment with the traumatized client in any book on cross-cultural social work practice. The orientation to treatment described in this chapter has evolved primarily out of the authors' understanding of Dr. Viktor Frankl's (1959) existential work with survivors of the Nazi death camps during and after World War II.

Many people in the United States experience post-traumatic stress reaction in response to initial trauma, even years before, that can cause symptoms which greatly distress survivors and their friends and families. Common symptoms such as depression, sleeplessness, flashback experiences, shame, fear, guilt, low self-esteem, somatic complaints, and rage are often seen as symptoms of post-traumatic stress (McNew and Abell, 1995; Sgroi and Bunk, 1988; Silver and Iacano, 1986). Trauma, experienced and expressed in rage and anger, brings frightening experiences to awareness but often in symbolic and representative ways. Experiences of post-traumatic stress disorder are equally frightening for the survivor whether the stimulus is war, abuse, severe and sudden injury, or some other equally terrorizing and traumatizing intrusion.

The purpose of this chapter is to outline the use of Frankl's (1959, 1988) existential treatment concepts in work with the traumatized client. In our opinion, Frankl's (1959) treatment approach with concentration camp survivors during and after World War II has special significance to a social work practitioner dealing with clients who have experienced trauma and terror. The authors also believe that Frankl's (1959, 1988) ideas about the human will to meaning are especially helpful when working with these clients as they try to cope with trauma and terror (Lantz, 1974, 1990, 1991, 1993; Lantz and Harper, 1990; Lantz and Lantz, 1991, 1992). The will to find meaning in life renews courage and the need to survive even in the face of very painful events.

Trauma and Repression

People who have been traumatized often use repression to keep from directly experiencing painful memories of trauma and terror (Lifton, 1973; Figley, 1990; Frankl, 1959; Lantz, 1974; Lantz and Greenlee, 1990). Such repression, however, is a double-edged process. On the one hand, it keeps the traumatized person from experiencing painful memories of trauma and terror (Figley; Lantz, 1990). On the other hand, it also helps to keep the person from experiencing the meaning potentials that are always embedded in an experience of trauma and terror (Frankl, 1959, 1975; Lantz, 1993). In this existential understanding of repression and terror, even the terror of a Nazi death camp includes some meaning potentials to be discovered and acted upon on a conscious level of awareness (Frankl, 1959, 1975).

The idea that memories that are repressed by a person also include meaning potentials that have been pulled into the unconscious during the repression of trauma and terror provides the traumatized client requesting help an unusual treatment opportunity (Lantz, 1993; Frankl, 1959; Lantz and Lantz, 1991). From this existential point of view, helping the traumatized client to remember traumatic and terrifying experiences can also be a way of helping the client to recover to consciousness meaning potentials that have been embedded in unconscious memories (Frankl, 1959; Lantz, 1993; Lantz and Harper, 1990). Thus, flashbacks and intrusive memories can be understood as methods the individual often uses to initiate a search for the meanings and meaning potentials embedded in the memories of terror (Frankl, 1975; Lantz, 1974, 1991, 1993; Williams, 1983; Tick, 1989; Lantz and Lantz, 1991).

The recovery to consciousness of meanings and meaning potentials that have been embedded in terror can be an extremely painful process for the traumatized individual (Lantz, 1974, 1990, 1991). Such a recovery of meaning awareness can often trigger powerful and dramatic treatment results (Frankl, 1959; Tick, 1989; Lantz, 1993). The remembering of trauma and terror without the recovery of meaning potentials to consciousness is often dangerous and extremely damaging to the client requesting help (Lantz, 1974, 1978, 1990, 1991, 1993; Lantz and Lantz, 1991). The two following case illustrations demonstrate the use of existential realization, control, and cleansing experiences during the process of cross-cultural social work with a traumatized client.

Mrs. S

Mrs. S served as an Army emergency surgery nurse in Vietnam during 1969 and 1970. She worked extremely long hours to save the lives of severely wounded American soldiers. Mrs. S requested social work treatment in 1975 after breast surgery and chemotherapy for cancer were unsuccessful and after learning her prognosis was terminal. She reported, "Since my surgery I have been having flashbacks where I see dying soldiers whom I worked on in Vietnam."

Mrs. S reported that she had had no difficulty in adjusting to civilian life after returning from Vietnam. She reported, "I never talked about Vietnam when I came home because no one wanted to listen." Mrs. S blocked out her Vietnam past. Mr. S reported that he had tried to talk to her about Vietnam but that she did not want to bring it up again. Mr. S admitted, "I didn't try real hard because I wasn't sure it was a good idea to stir things up."

In this situation, a 33-year-old ex-Army nurse who had been exposed to the terrible gore and death associated with Vietnam combat wounds was unable to talk about her experiences when she first came home. Fifteen years later, facing death from cancer, she began to get in touch with her Vietnam past. For Mrs. S, flashbacks served the function of "making me think about Vietnam before I die." Social work treatment with the S family focused upon using reflection experiences to help Mrs. S and her family talk about her Vietnam memories, to help her "grieve the young men I lost in Vietnam," and, in her daughter's words, "to help us honor Mom for the job she did in Vietnam" (cleansing and existential realization). The social worker helped the family realize that sharing Mrs. S's Vietnam past could be a meaningful way of helping the children remember "Mom with pride" as they faced the conflicts of adolescence without a mother (control).

Mrs. T

Mrs. T requested treatment after she started having "terrifying images of small and crowding-in space, with creeping bugs and only splashes of light just as I fall asleep." These images triggered anxiety and Mrs. T had started drinking to help her fall asleep. Mrs. T described the images as having started after her daughter's seventh birthday.

In this clinical situation, Mrs. T started having flashback images of her own seventh year of life when she had been repeatedly raped and sodomized by a relative, an uncle who told her that he would kill her mother if she told her mother what he had done to her. The uncle stayed with her family for three months while recovering from a broken ankle.

Mrs. T tearfully recalled having told her mother that her uncle "chased me in the dark and locked me naked in the cupboard under the kitchen sink where the roaches lived," but her mother had called her a "crazy girl" because she believed her brother more than her daughter. Mrs. T remembered her mother saying, "Your uncle couldn't ever run with his poor ankle and would not do such a dirty trick anyway." Mrs. T apparently then had repressed these memories of terror until her own daughter, aged seven, had been playing house and hiding her dolls amidst the pots and pans under the kitchen sink at home.

Social work treatment with Mrs. T focused upon helping her to remember and talk out her terror at the hands of her uncle (cleansing and worldview respect). First, she talked with her husband to try to think why her parents had refused to help her as a child. With her husband's and the social worker's support, Mrs.

T invited her mother into family treatment to tell her what she remembered and to ask her why her plea for help had been ignored.

Mrs. T discovered that her mother had not known what to do as she loved her brother and doubted that he would ever do "such horrible, dirty things." She had convinced herself that her daughter's story was only the result of imagination of a seven-year-old child. Mrs. T's mother admitted that she had not told Mrs. T's father because "your Dad never liked my brother. He always called him a freeloader who couldn't be trusted. Now your Dad's dead and I can't tell him."

Mrs. T was surprised to discover her mother's considerable support for her as well as anger toward her uncle, who had died several years prior to Mrs. T's rediscovery of her trauma from age seven. Mrs. T discovered her aged mother to be extremely sorry and to admit that she "felt awful for not believing my own child at a time when she needed me most." Her mother was remorseful for having allowed her daughter to suffer alone.

Mrs. and Mr. T reported that perhaps the most helpful part of treatment was the way the social worker helped them develop a plan to find meaning in Mrs. T's experience of terror and sexual abuse (existential realization). After reliving her own time of terror, Mrs. T was able to transcend her own pain through helping others by volunteering with a child abuse prevention program that taught children to understand "good touches" and "bad touches" and to report such experiences to parents, teachers, and others in their lives. Mrs. T reported that this volunteer work was a practical way by which she could make her past mean something. She was able to share experiences from her volunteer work with her husband and to find new meaning in their marriage (existential realization).

Mr. T was able to learn to give support to his wife during her time of remembering the abuse. Together they talked with her mother to clarify the details of Mrs. T's rape and molestation when she was only seven. Mrs. T was absolved of any feelings of failure on her part to protect herself and felt somewhat relieved that her mother saw her failure to protect her child as her own mistake because she was afraid to confront her brother (cleansing).

Stages in Social Work with Traumatized Clients

As we review the two previous clinical illustrations, we note that such a brief clinical review could give the impression that social work treatment with traumatized clients is a short-term treatment approach. In our opinion, this is not the case. In the S illustration, treatment lasted from three months before the death of Mrs. S to seven months afterward, nearly 10 months in all. The S family was in treatment for almost two years. In our experience, social work treatment with traumatized people is most often a somewhat lengthy process. In our opinion, the process of treatment includes five stages as described below.

Stage One: Establishing the Treatment System

In the first stage of social work treatment with the traumatized client, the client and social worker focus upon developing trust and commitment to the treatment process (worldview respect) (Andrews, 1974; Figley, 1990; Lantz, 1993). Traumatized clients may spend a considerable amount of time testing to see whether the social worker will be able to help them manage their memories of trauma and terror in a safe and empathic way (Lantz, 1974, 1991). Such testing is largely unconscious. Lindy (1988) describes this unconscious testing as "securing the perimeter" when it is manifested by Vietnam veterans. In our opinion, the traumatized client is generally very wise in selecting a social worker. The client can often unconsciously feel whether a given social work professional will be able to work with the client's specific experiences of terror. A social worker should not be expected to be able to work with every traumatized client and should respect a client's desire to work with a different helper without blaming the client or viewing their resistance as pathological (Lantz, 1974, 1978, 1993; Lantz and Lantz, 1991, 1992). The match between client and social worker is particularly important in situations of past episodes involving trauma (Lantz and Lantz, 1992).

Stage Two: Remembering Terror

In stage two, the social worker helps the client remember the specific details of the trauma (cleansing). The client is encouraged to examine the traumatic event or events in detail and to reflect upon how the trauma has disrupted and affected his or her life (Lantz, 1974, 1978, 1991, 1993). The client is also encouraged to reflect upon how trauma has disrupted meaning opportunities and the awareness of meaning potentials in his or her life (existential realization) (Lantz, 1974, 1993; Lantz and Harper, 1989; Lantz and Lantz, 1991, 1992).

In stage two, the social worker helps the client remember the traumatic events in as much detail as possible. The client is encouraged to tell his or her story of the trauma in a way that often includes sight, sound, taste, smell, and tactile experiences as well as their reactions to the trauma (Lantz, 1974, 1993). The more detail that can be remembered and talked out, the greater the possibility that the client will be able to discover meaning potentials in their story of trauma and terror during stage three.

Stage Three: Recovering Meaning in Trauma and Terror

In our experience, stages two and three are difficult to separate in actual social work practice. Separation appears in this chapter only for the purpose of clarity. In stage three, the social worker facilitates the client's recovery of meaning opportunities that were embedded in the memories of trauma and terror (existential realization and control) (Lantz, 1974, 1978, 1993). In our opinion, the traumatized client will not be able to recover fully without finding a way to reframe the experience as a meaning potential (control and existential realization) (Lantz, 1993; Frankl, 1959). We strongly agree with Frankl (1959) who reports that victims of terror can recover most fully when they find a way to make use of the self-transcendent meaning opportunities that evolve out of the traumatic experience. Frankl (1959, 1988) has consistently pointed out that many victims of holocaust terror were able to realize their human potential fully only after discovering a personally unique way of giving to the world that evolved out of their personal concentration camp experiences and memories of terror. Frankl's (1959) ideas about the self-transcendent use of the personal experience of trauma and terror as a means of finding a way to give to the world have also been described by Lifton (1973) in his work with atomic-bomb survivors and Vietnam veterans, and by Lantz (1991, 1993) in his work with Vietnam veteran family groups. Both clients in the case illustrations provided earlier in this chapter were able to discover meaning opportunities for giving to the world that had been embedded in family memories of terror (existential realization).

Memories of terror may also facilitate meaning discovery by helping to explain a specific client symptom or symptom cluster. Often victims of terror develop unusual symptoms that they experience as "crazy." Helping the traumatized client to discover the meaning of a symptom can often greatly decrease anxiety, improve self-esteem, and help them to realize that they are not crazy (control) (Lantz and Lantz, 1991, 1992).

Stage Four: Making Use of Meaning Potentials

In stage four, the social work practitioner helps the client make use of the meaning potentials embedded in trauma and terror that were recovered to consciousness in stages two and three. This "making use" of trauma and terror is most effective when it occurs through self-transcendent giving to the world (Frankl, 1959). Such giving can occur in a self-transcendent relationship with nature, with an important cause, or with other human beings (Frankl, 1959, 1975). Frankl (1959, 1988) believes that such self-transcendent giving is the only effective way to transform survivor's guilt into survivor's responsibility.

Frankl's (1959, 1975) concept of meaning discovery through self-transcendent giving to the world has been stated in a different way by Lifton (1973) in his work with survivors of a near-death situation. Lifton consistently points out that survivors of a near-death experience have two major possible responses to the personal brush with death. Lifton believes that people can go "numb" and repress the experience of near-death and its associated anxiety at the expense of a full and rich life in the here and now, or the person can fully experience death anxiety and let this anxiety evolve into creativity and advocacy. Frankl (1959, 1975) would clearly agree with Lifton's point, but would label the responses of creativity and advocacy as self-transcendent giving to the world.

In the daily, practical world of social work with traumatized clients, it is the social worker's task to help the client find his or her own ways to transform terror into meaning through creative activities and activities of advocacy (Lantz, 1974, 1987, 1991; Lantz and Lantz, 1991). The following clinical material illustrates how this might be done.

The U Family

Mr. U served in Vietnam in 1966 and 1967. When he returned home, he married his high school girlfriend. He graduated from college in 1971. Mr. and Mrs. U's son, William, Jr., was born in 1970. Mr. U experienced no problems in adjusting to life at home after returning from Vietnam. After being home for 15 years, he started having flashbacks and intrusive memories about his time in Vietnam. Social work reflection with Mr. and Mrs. U helped Mr. U remember Vietnam. He told his wife about killing a Viet Cong soldier in a firefight who was about the same age as his son and about his platoon finding a peasant village in a free-fire zone that was destroyed by American bombing (cleansing). In this clinical situation, Mr. and Mrs. U used these memories of terror as reasons to become better parents to William, Jr., and to become active as volunteers at a shelter for the homeless in honor of the dead young soldier and Mr. U's "village memory" (cleansing, control, and existential realization).

Stage Five: Celebration and Termination

In stage five the social work practitioner helps the traumatized client establish and maintain a natural social network of support and meaning, helps the client celebrate the changes made during social work treatment, and helps them terminate treatment (control, rites of initiation) (Lantz, 1974, 1978, 1987, 1990, 1993; Lantz and Lantz, 1991, 1992).

In our opinion, celebration and termination should not occur until the client has had a comfortable period of time to integrate the newly discovered meanings into daily life. Premature attempts at both celebration and termination generally result in a recurrence of the symptoms that brought the traumatized client into treatment. An effective method for both the client and the social worker to judge whether or not the client is ready to terminate treatment is to observe carefully the emotional quality of a "pre-termination celebration" (Lantz, 1978, 1990; Lantz and Lantz, 1991).

A pre-termination celebration is a celebration of separation. It is planned by the client and social worker and often includes snacks, coffee, and soft drinks. The social worker should be especially alert to the emotional quality of the separation celebration, making sure it is both emotional and spontaneous and making sure that there is an ambiance of joy and sadness, excitement and regret. All members of the separating treatment situation should be emotionally involved in the pre-termination celebration (Lantz, 1978, 1993; Lantz and Lantz, 1991).

If the pre-termination celebration is experienced by either the client or the social worker as a forced or hollow occasion, termination is possibly premature (Lantz, 1978, 1993). If it does not include mixed feelings of anxiety, joyful anticipation, and lingering regret, termination is probably not indicated (Lantz, 1990, 1991, 1993). In such a situation the social worker should talk openly about these concerns with the traumatized client. An informed and mutual decision about termination may then be reached.

Conclusion

In this chapter we have described the potential for violence that is present in the United States, and we have offered a five-stage social work treatment system that has great potential to help the traumatized client master the experience of trauma and terror. The approach has been found useful with many traumatized clients, and its usefulness has been documented in a wide variety of clinical studies (Lantz, 1991, 1993; Lantz and Lantz, 1991).

CHAPTER TEN

Gay and Lesbian Clients

Before a social work practitioner attempts to provide service to gay and lesbian clients, the social worker should have already examined and worked through his or her own sexual identity issues, homophobia, and attitudes toward the gay and lesbian population (Shernoff, 1984; Loewenstein, 1980; Brown, 1989). Brown and others (Hall, 1978; Krestan and Bepko, 1980; Loewenstein) point out that homophobia is deeply ingrained in our culture and that it is not at all unusual for straight social workers to discover in the middle of work with a gay or lesbian client that they are having serious negative countertransference problems that disrupt their ability to provide adequate, empathic, and professional services to the client.

It is not clear why homophobia is so deeply ingrained in our culture. Tully and Nibao (1979) believe that homophobia in the United States has been promoted and prescribed by religious traditions that have evolved out of the Old Testament, and that such homophobic attitudes have been woven into our legal system through legislation banning the commission of homosexual acts. Rich (1983) believes that homophobia is a part of the paternalistic economic system in the United States that helps to control women.

Legislation against homosexual acts in the United States and the prevailing homophobic elements in our culture have helped many gay and lesbian persons feel great fear about revealing their sexual orientation and have facilitated a pattern where many gay men and lesbian women remain covert about their sexual practices (Tully and Nibao, 1979).

For many years, homosexuality was considered to be a mental illness or an emotional problem by many psychiatrists, psychologists, and social workers in the United States (Loewenstein, 1980).

Homosexuality has been considered by the psychiatric establishment not to be a mental illness unless a person wants to change his or her gay or lesbian sexual orientation (Gregory and Smeltzer, 1977). In spite of this change in the diagnostic and classification system of the American Psychiatric Association, the mental health community still harbors considerable hostility, prejudice, and hatred against gay men and lesbian women (Hall, 1978; Loewenstein; Shernoff, 1984; Brown, 1989).

Gay men and lesbian women are different from heterosexuals in two distinct ways. First, they experience more disrespect and hatred from the mainstream community than do heterosexual persons and they experience considerable stress because of such hatred (Brown, 1989). Second, gay men and lesbian women tend to be more interested in having intimate and sexual relationships with persons of the same gender than do heterosexual persons. These two differences in no way change the important fact that there is tremendous heterogeneity within the gay and lesbian community. Gay men and lesbian women come from all races, ethnic backgrounds, geographical areas, and socioeconomic levels. They can be mentally healthy or have emotional problems, just as do heterosexual individuals. According to Rothblum (1990), there is evidence that lesbians are no different in psychological adjustment in general than heterosexual women. Actually, the stress placed on lesbian women by homophobic pressures in society requires considerable resiliency and coping strengths.

Gay men and lesbian women may be liberal or conservative, religiously oriented or nonreligious. They reflect all of the differences that exist among people who are alive and well in the world today. There is no way at present to know how many gay and lesbian persons live in the United States, since many are not willing to share this aspect of their lives with public officials or census workers; however, a frequent estimate is that one in twelve Americans is gay or lesbian (Rothblum, 1990).

Working with Gay and Lesbian Clients

We are of the opinion that the most important element of cross-cultural social work practice with the special population of gay and lesbian clients is to be aware of the potential damage done to their self-esteem by the hatred shown to them by the dominant culture (Hall, 1978). Many gay men and lesbian women are very aware that to openly express their true self to society is dangerous and opens the self to the probability of being hurt (Loewenstein, 1980). As a result, many gay men and lesbian women may be hesitant to openly reveal their sexual orientation to the heterosexual social worker and may engage in testing behavior to see whether the social worker can be trusted to be accepting and empathic (Moses and Hawkins, 1982). We recommend that the cross-cultural social work practitioner view such testing behavior as functional, rational, and a client strength.

A second important concept in social work with gay and lesbian clients is to understand that they often have problems that have little or nothing to do with their sexual orientation. For example, if a gay or lesbian client requests counseling for depression, the depression may or may not be linked to the client's sexual orientation. It is a mistake and often a manifestation of the helper's homophobia when the social worker sees all of the client's problems as being a reaction to the client's sexual orientation or to the hatred the client experiences from the dominant culture.

Third, in social work practice with gay and lesbian clients, it is important for the worker to understand that referral resources the worker usually trusts and utilizes during network intervention with heterosexual clients may not be as helpful with gay and lesbian clients. Homophobic attitudes of individuals in the social worker's referral network may interfere with service delivery (Moses and Hawkins, 1982). As a result, the practitioner should make every attempt to assess the levels of prejudice shown toward gay and lesbian persons by the referral resources the worker often utilizes in his or her daily practice (Lantz and Lenahan, 1976).

A fourth important theme in social work practice with gay men and lesbian women is sometimes called the problem of "fusion." The problem of fusion has been called a problem of separation-individuation by some object-relationship therapists and a cohesion-independence issue by some existential therapists (Lantz, 1978). Without regard to sexual orientation, all persons must deal with the problem of fusion, or what the authors call the cohesion-independence issue (Lantz, 1978, 1993).

In the cohesion-independence issue of human existence, the person is viewed as naturally and normally undergoing a life cycle of two constantly alternating processes. These processes are being close and cohesive for support and emotional nurturance and then being apart and separate for autonomy and independent responsibility (Andrews, 1974; Lantz, 1978). This human existential issue is neither a lesbian, nor gay, nor straight issue. It occurs in all human living. Each individual must learn to be alone and separate as part of the growth of self-esteem and the person's capacity for self-care. At the same time, each person must also learn to be cohesive and close to other persons for the purpose of learning to be intimate and self-transcendent. In normal human growth and development, the person's family, social network, and community provide opportunities to develop the "real self" through cohesion experiences in which the person learns to be close, and separation experiences in which the person learns to be independent (Andrews; Lantz, 1978). Gay and lesbian persons learn early that to "come out" and be the "real self" is, in fact, an act that will place them at risk for rejection and even hatred by some people. As a result some gay men and lesbian women are not able to find support for the real self within their family of origin, with childhood friends, or within the family of origin's social network. In such a situation the individual may be forced to find support for the real self *only* in the gay and lesbian community (Krestan and Bepko, 1980). At a later time the individual may find it difficult to manifest aspects of the real self that do not fit the norms and expectations of the gay and lesbian community. The individual may feel afraid to "individuate" as doing so may cost them the emotional and social support of the gay and lesbian community (Krestan and Bepko). Again, in our view this issue of cohesion and independence is an existential and developmental problem for all persons, not just gay men and lesbian women.

In addition to the cohesion-independence issue of human existence, the curative factors approach is useful in the process of helping the gay or lesbian couple to accept and manifest the real self. The process of coming out has the potential for both great joy and great despair for both gay men and lesbian women. Many find the results of finally coming out to be a profound joy in that it feels very good to no longer "hide and feel ashamed of the real person that I am." On the other hand, "coming out puts you in danger. It lets you find out which friends will stay with you and which ones will treat you like you got the plague" (Anonymous, 1990). For many gay men and lesbian women, the process of coming out includes considerable pain as many old friends are no longer willing to remain friends and many family members and childhood friends are unwilling to provide acceptance. In spite of its potential for great pain and sadness, many gay men and lesbian women view the process of coming out as a liberating, almost life-saving, activity (Anonymous; Moses and Hawkins, 1982). To no longer feel ashamed, to be part of an accepting community, and to discover "islands of freedom where you can be yourself can take a tremendous load off your shoulders" (Anonymous). Despite the terror of having family and friends know about sexual orientation, the most common volunteer effort in response to the spread of AIDS has been family members of gay and lesbian people, some with AIDS relatives (Kayal, 1994).

The authors of this book believe that the decision to come out, to accept one's lesbian or gay identity, is a tremendously important life event for gay men and lesbian women. The heterosexual social worker should not attempt to work with this clinical situation without great knowledge of the gay and lesbian community and without good consultation and supervision from a qualified gay or lesbian practitioner.

Finally, the fear of contracting AIDS is known by people of heterosexual orientation but is an even greater fear among gay and lesbian populations. At the present time, regardless of sexual orientation, all persons are at considerable risk for contracting this deadly disease. Gay men and intravenous drug users are presently at an increased risk for contracting AIDS, although this is rapidly changing. It is a rare gay or lesbian individual who does not know someone who is dying or has died from AIDS. Because gay men and lesbian women have a tradition of being supportive toward each other in the face of discrimination by the dominant culture, many lesbian women also have been affected by the death of a friend from AIDS.

HIV or AIDS-Affected Clients

Fear, hate, and anger toward gay and lesbian populations, particularly those with sexually acquired HIV or AIDS, represent social and political constraints that preclude full inclusion of primary health care for HIV/AIDS patients. The authors of this book agree with many gay men and lesbian women who believe that inadequate federal money presently being spent on AIDS research probably results from the hatred felt toward gay men and lesbian women by the dominant culture. Such policy and funding decisions are manifestations of societal attitudes and biases. Humanistic and compassionate services are seriously needed, particularly in cases of women and persons of color who are victims of AIDS (Norman and Dumois, 1995).

Long-term survivors with AIDS experience the need to make accommodations around jobs, drugs, self-esteem needs, and self-nurturance needs. It has been noted that long-term survivors of AIDS have found meaning in life, cope actively with their illness, and take great responsibility for living, being, and doing (Jue, 1994).

Loss, loneliness, and isolation are commonly experienced by long-term survivors of AIDS (Jue, 1994). The grief felt by many gay men and lesbian women in reaction to the loss of a good friend from AIDS is a common occurrence and is often an important focus area in cross-cultural practice with gay men and lesbian women.

Marital Therapy with Gay Men and Lesbian Women

A frequently requested service that many gay men and lesbian women want from social work practitioners is "marital therapy" or "relationship therapy." The literature about marital or relationship therapy with gay men and lesbian women is not extensive, although a few excellent articles have appeared in recent years (Shernoff, 1984).

In 1975 the second author organized a three-day panel discussion workshop sponsored by the Southwest Mental Health Center in Columbus, Ohio, where three gay couples and three lesbian couples who had been successfully together in what they referred to as "marital relationships" for over ten years talked to mental health practitioners about healthy gay and lesbian marriages and what marital therapy with gay and lesbian couples should try to accomplish (Lantz, 1975). All six couples reported that they had used traditional marital therapy services at one time or another over the course of their "marriage" to help them to work out problems. The couples reported that the marital therapist had been straight and that the "marital therapy" had been helpful. The following themes emerged and reemerged over the three-day workshop.

The first theme that emerged and reemerged during this workshop was that the six couples reported that the hatred and disrespect shown to gay or lesbian couples by the dominant straight cultural majority can help the members of the couple to feel "bad," "evil," "crazy," and "sick." All in the group believed that the therapist should in some way help the couple learn to "cleanse themselves" of the toxic messages they so frequently receive from the dominant culture (Lantz, 1975).

A second theme that emerged and reemerged was that the marital therapist should be aware that the members of the gay or lesbian relationship have learned to hide their true feelings and show a false face to the dominant culture, and that gay and lesbian couples often use this skill with each other to avoid conflict and the manifestation of problems. All six couples stated that the therapist needs to help gay and lesbian couples learn that this avoidance skill, which is often helpful when dealing with the dominant culture, is often very damaging when used within the gay or lesbian relationship (Lantz, 1975).

A third theme that emerged and reemerged during the workshop was that all of the couples believed that the therapist should accept responsibility for knowing other professionals and service givers who are not homophobic. The therapist should be responsible not to refer a gay or lesbian couple to homophobic community resources and that such a responsibility means that the therapist should check out the level of homophobia of community services and agency representatives (Lantz, 1975).

A fourth theme that emerged in the workshop had to do with homophobic countertransference reactions. All six couples reported that in their minds their own personal marital therapist had been "slightly homophobic" and at times expressed such homophobic attitudes (Lantz, 1975). The couples believed that what had helped them and their therapist to overcome the therapist's homophobic countertransference reactions was the therapist's openness and willingness to admit that he or she might have some homophobic issues. This openness on the part of the therapist seemed to help the couples to work through the problems in a more open and trusting way.

A final issue reported by all six couples was the cohesion-independence issue. They reported thinking that at times they had become too dependent upon each other and that such dependence and reliance upon the other for emotional support created problems in manifesting the independent side of the person. All of the couples stated that the dominant culture's hostility toward gay men and lesbian women tended to push them to rely only upon each other and to become too dependent (Lantz, 1975).

A Case Illustration: Ms. K and Ms. S

Ms. K and Ms. S requested marital therapy at a community mental health center. They wanted to improve their relationship and had been referred for marital therapy by a priest at a Roman Catholic church in Columbus, Ohio. The couple had had a marital ceremony four years earlier and considered themselves to be married.

The couple complained of frequent (but unsuccessful) arguments, a less than satisfactory sexual relationship, and a recognition that both partners were wanting to spend more and more time away from each other. Ms. K was in law school, Ms. S was a teacher, and both stated that they had been having problems for about two years. The couple exhibited a relationship interactional style that included an overly intellectualizing partner (Ms. K) and a partner who either withdrew or "acted up" to deal with problems (Ms. S). Both members of the relationship used a number of interactional methods to avoid intimacy.

Ms. K and Ms. S both appeared to be extremely ambivalent about their relationship. On one hand, both members of the relationship wanted to keep it going but both also felt smothered and controlled. Both Ms. K and Ms. S had some concerns about being in a treatment relationship with a male heterosexual social worker but both reported that they wanted services from this worker because of his good reputation and his past experience doing marital and relationship therapy with gay and lesbian couples.

The treatment approach used by the social worker with the client couple was "experiential" and used the time and space of the conjoint treatment session to help the couple notice and become aware of the communication "cut offs" that they used to avoid friction. The couple was also helped to notice that by avoiding conflict they were also avoiding the intimacy which generally follows the resolution and working through of conflict. The social worker was active and direct with the couple in a way that challenged their avoidance and helped them "stick with it" when they wanted to "cut out" from their problems and conflicts.

In addition to helping this couple openly manifest, discuss, and resolve conflicts during this couple's treatment interview, this worker also gave the couple a variety of nonverbal intimacy exercises (for example, holding hands and using pressure in the hands to express feelings) that they could use to get back in touch with their positive feelings towards each other. These nonverbal exercises stimulated additional theories to be talked out during treatment.

Ms. K and Ms. S were seen seventeen times in conjoint relationship therapy over a six-month period of time. The couple reported good progress and reported that relationship therapy had been of tremendous help.

Curative Factors with Ms. K and Ms. S

Both Ms. K and Ms. S reported that the social worker's openness to his own ignorance and lack of knowledge about the gay and lesbian community coupled with his confidence in his knowledge about relationship therapy was refreshing and gave them hope. The couple reported that the nonverbal exercises helped them discover and express feelings (cleansing) and that the communication training in the conjoint interviews helped them feel more "control." The final factor considered important by this couple was the respect that the therapist gave to them and their experiences as members of a special population (worldview respect).

Conclusion

Gay men and lesbian women live in a dominant homophobic society that creates great stress for the gay or lesbian person. Cross-cultural social workers who work with gay men and lesbian women should constantly monitor the homophobic attitudes of the culture-at-large and any elements of that culture that reside within the cross-cultural practitioner that are manifested in homophobic countertransference reactions. The recent onset of HIV or AIDS has created additional stress and anxiety for gay and lesbian populations in their homosexual orientation and relationships.

Working with HIV- or AIDS-affected clients requires crisis services in the early stages and a broad variety of individual and family intervention skills (Greene, Kropf, and MacNair, 1994). Cross-cultural curative factors such as helper attractiveness, cleansing experiences which can assist with acceptance and improved self-image, existential realization or the potential to discover new meaning in life, and physical intervention at different levels of health care needs are important. Perhaps even more important in the face of the deadly disorder of AIDS is the curative factor of hope, where positive potentials for healing can produce healing in body and in spirit for the victim.

CHAPTER ELEVEN

Women Clients

The American woman is perhaps the most diverse symbol of today's culturally pluralist world. She is well-educated; a professional in scientific fields, a nurse, a teacher, a doctor, self-employed, or supervising others; and economically advantaged. She is also poor, illiterate, and has never been employed. She is a person of many colors, many languages, married, single, old, and young. As a bearer of various cultures, she is complete with "knowing." She knows foods, dress, values, holidays, work, folk medicine, and family roles consistent with her heritage. Nevertheless, despite wide personal differences, women in America have experienced great commonality in gender discrimination and oppression in the social and political contexts of their lives (Harper, 1990b, 1991).

The plight of women in America needs to be investigated in order to gain understanding and to develop a resolution for change that not only offers hope for economic and social equality but enhances satisfaction in personal life. Many women experience multiple victimizations and become unserved victims. Others receive restitution or treatment for a single episode of victimization or discrimination that is agreed to warrant some sort of treatment of the victim and sometimes punishment of the offender. Social, political, and economic boundaries isolate women and shield their victimization from common understanding. Multiple sources of victimization produce a multiplicity of injustices, including poverty, single-parenthood, unemployment, powerlessness, and low self-esteem. Many women have been victims of sexual abuse, physical abuse by parents or family members, or battering by a husband. From a feminist perspective, abuse of women is a metaphor for patriarchal control of women (Hanmer and Statham, 1989). Direct physical violence in families or by individuals known to the victim is extremely detrimental to women in their search for direction and meaning in life.

Feminist analyses of the sociocultural milieu and the socialization of women in America are needed to evaluate the extent of gender socialization for women in both rural and urban settings. This chapter discusses the origin and interrelatedness of economic, social, and political factors that contribute to the victimization of women. Strategies for practice with American women will be explored from a feminist perspective and case examples will be provided. The reality-based orientation underpinning much social work intervention is particularly appropriate in helping women to restore a sense of meaning in their lives after experiences of oppression and even severe abuse. Gender oppression is experienced by women throughout much of the world, regardless of racial or cultural heritage.

Feminist Thought: Existential, Liberal, Socialist, and Radical Perspectives

Simone de Beauvoir (1968) explained that "male" is often viewed as a positive force in culture and that "female" is often viewed in culture as a negative force. By relegating women to "subject" existence, the patriarchy has defined cultural, economic, and political statuses of women in society. Informed by existentialist philosophers such as Hegel, Hasserl, Heidegger, and Sartre, de Beauvoir placed personal transcendence above biological forces. De Beauvoir described gender distinctions in a patriarchal social context as being misdefined as fundamental to reproduction and to identity (Donovan, 1987). She saw the path to women's transcendence over domination and subjugation as being creativity and performance through work. Such transcendence, however, becomes a moral journey involving a new sense of being in the world and even a time of experiencing a changed sense of marginality in the emergent process of overcoming the role of object and discovering self (Donovan; de Beauvoir).

Class and gender oppression are interrelated spheres of oppression (Eisenstein, 1984). Women's present occupations and economic contributions have been devalued in America, especially in areas where the women's movement is less evident. For many poor women, the women's movement has not been an important part of their reality. For women separated from the women's movement, their lack of a feminist lens through which to view their social and economic situation is part of their oppression.

Historically, a woman who worked outside her family was giving a signal that her husband was a poor provider (Burgess, 1994). Work for economic productivity was frowned upon with the result that middle- and upper-class women poured their energies into philanthropic movements in England and in America. The combination of race and gender is particularly telling in view of African American women who were brought as workers and assigned slave status (Burgess; Aguilar and Williams, 1993). Hispanic women, likely to be poor because of their increasing numbers and educational needs as well as recency of migration, have expected roles in their family, but lack clarity in their public role (Aguilar and Williams).

Minority women in America are challenged to find identity and meaning in their lives while confronted by sexism and racism along with great risk for poverty and oppression. The decline of wages and employment among African American and Puerto Rican males contributes to poverty of women and children in these populations and places a greater burden on women for financial support (Starrels, Bould, and Nicholas, 1994). In the Puerto Rican culture, women are to be more "self-sacrificing" and to have power through mothering and traditional homemaker roles (Green, 1995). Different perspectives for understanding roles and statuses of women focus on the interface of the woman and society and of her struggle in political, economic, and personal spheres.

The liberal feminist perspective places importance on protecting women's reproductive role and allows women to struggle for equal opportunity. Liberal theory does not call for changing the present political, social, or economic structure of society (Friedan, 1986). Liberal feminists identify patriarchal values and traditionally male-dominated institutions as causes of female oppression (Freeman, 1984). Gender inequities include denial of rights, gender discrimination in education and employment opportunities, and relegation to child care and homemaking activities (Tong, 1989). In promoting human equality, liberalism emphasizes liberty and opposes political, economic, and social hierarchies (Abramovitz, 1988). The goal of liberal feminists is to resolve sexual inequality through reducing barriers and preventing discrimination (Tong). As a reform movement, liberal feminism seeks equal access through legal redress rather than a revolutionary restructuring of the social order (Shillito, 1990).

Socialist feminism attempts to define gender roles in contemporary society. Socialist feminists identify capitalism and patriarchy as the root causes of female oppression (Abramovitz, 1988). In the socialist feminist theoretical orientation, female oppression stems both from the capitalist class and property system and from male-dominated power relations. The resultant division of labor is based on production (male/public sphere) and reproduction (female/private sphere) (Nes and Iadicola, 1989). As defined by patriarchal capitalism, roles of women and men are representative of their gender positions within the social order.

According to socialist feminists, patriarchal social relationships exclude women from the public sphere and restrict them to the private sphere (Jaggar, 1983). Particularly relevant to those living in poverty, women contribute unpaid labor in the private sphere where women's roles are in childbearing, family nurturance, and food production in support of families. The productive activities of women have the side effect of benefitting capitalism. Women then remain dependent and powerless because their productive contributions are defined as "women's work" by employed males who occupy patriarchally defined social strata within the socioeconomic class system that dominates the American scene. Women who are caught in this situation cannot envision personal or political potential for themselves or others (Shillito, 1990).

Socialist feminism provides a framework for viewing how capitalistic patriarchy drives and reinforces the victimization of women (Shillito, 1990). The criticism that the socialist feminist analysis most clearly portrays the victimization of middle-class women (Abramovitz, 1988) is an important consideration for rural regions such as Appalachia where poverty is so intrusive. Racial, ethnic, and class differences of oppressed groups of women reduce the distinction between private and public productivity. Socialist feminism explains the influence of patriarchy in traditional, socioeconomically deprived regions. According to this theory, oppression may be overcome by establishing mutual respect, by fostering joint efforts of women and men to eliminate oppression, and by establishing more androgynous roles in society.

Radical feminists call for changing the way equality is created in society (Eisenstein, 1984). Reproduction and caregiving are valued as less important than work in the public arena. Radical feminists advocate creation of a social structure where all persons are truly equal, where women have the task of childbearing but do not necessarily have the burden of childrearing or caregiving (Spakes, 1989). Changing the balance of power in a patriarchal society requires drastic social upheaval, even revolution, as the male power holders are extremely reluctant to relinquish their power to women.

A feminist orientation offers a lens through which to view female oppression and provides a framework for understanding and modifying personal and social injustices. Feminism is concerned with ending domination and resisting oppression (Van Den Bergh and Cooper, 1986). As a political ideology liberating all oppressed persons, feminism extends to concerns not only of women, but also of those who are oppressed because of color, age, ethnicity, religion, and other special group membership.

Domination of women results in their oppression in both private and public spheres. Personally intrusive and victimizing, oppression is a major barrier to empowerment. Unable to escape patriarchal control, many women are victimized in a variety of ways. First, childhood sexual abuse causes great harm to its victims; second, wife abuse does physical and emotional damage; third, poverty destroys opportunities and expectations of women; and fourth, patriarchal control of women does violence to their spirits. A comprehensive feminist orientation is helpful in developing strategies to bring about social change for gender equality for all American women.

Implications for Social Work Practice

Poverty, disempowerment, and traditional sex-role socialization have negatively impacted both women and men. Few attempts have been made to understand the mechanisms by which individuals "make sense" of oppressive conditions when they choose "not to revolt" (Ferraro, 1983). Nevertheless, the continuing oppression of American women is a major concern.

The feminist pursuit of equality and justice is a long-term effort. Certainly, feminist thought has become a major force in the social work profession's response to women's oppression. It is recognized that feminist efforts have enabled many victims of gender oppression to become survivors (Friedan, 1986). The profession that is often closest to the problems of victimization and oppression of American women is social work.

A major thrust of feminist practice with women who live in America is action for social change. Consistent with socialist feminism, social work practitioners need to examine the social order that sets women apart by class and gender (Nes and Iadicola, 1989). Through consciousness-raising efforts and coalition building, women can gain power. The imbalance of public and private membership and rewards can be addressed from joint efforts toward androgyny in both private and public spheres (Harper, 1990b, 1991; Harper and Shillito, 1990). Van Den Bergh and Cooper (1986) have identified five principles of feminist social work practice as eliminating false dichotomies, reconceptualizing power, valuing process equally with product, honoring the validity of naming personal experience, and remembering that the personal is also political. They encourage social workers to incorporate these empowering principles into their work with female clients.

Consistent with feminism, social work practice functions can help establish equal opportunity for American women. One practice function is to help women in identifying gender roles that are characteristic of the socioeconomic situation in which they live. A second practice function, particularly important for socioeconomically disadvantaged clients, is to develop self-help or support groups for women to share experiences and begin to reshape some of the restrictive roles they occupy (Harper, 1986). For example, learning to develop and utilize alternate caregivers can be truly empowering for a woman who has little respite from caring for children or caring for elderly or ill relatives (Riemenschneider and Harper, 1990). A third social work function is to assist women with opportunities to participate in the public or production arena—this includes job training, employment, and education.

By gaining enough personal power to break the barriers to equality, women may participate more in the public sphere.

Finally, a fourth practice function requiring sensitivity on the part of the practitioner is to help survivors of childhood sexual abuse to overcome the damage this violation of their personal boundaries does to their lives. Many survivors of violent abuse have no memory of the abuse itself and lead lives full of hopelessness, despair, and failure. Unaware of the source of their problem, with low self-esteem and unable to set personal goals, these clients may present a wide variety of symptoms. Such symptoms include alcoholism, drug abuse, general depression, blocked creativity, or eating disorders such as compulsive overeating, bulimia, or anorexia nervosa (Lantz and Lantz, 1992; Harper and Shillito, 1991). From a clinical perspective, victims of trauma such as sexual assault often utilize repression to avoid directly experiencing the pain of terror again (Lifton, 1973; Frankl, 1953; Lantz and Lantz, 1991). Protected by repression, the victim avoids exposure to trauma awareness but is also unable to fully experience meaning potentials that are embedded in the trauma. Exploring the trauma helps the victim to recover lost meaning potentials and to have courage to experience feelings and reach out to help others (Lantz and Lantz, 1991, 1992).

Feminist Social Work Practice with Two Rural Women

Victimization and oppression of rural women often reflect values and attitudes that are linked intergenerationally. Particular constraints of the familial system often maintain a woman and man in a marriage sanctioned by patriarchal values that are supported by rural cultural traditions. Such values in many rural areas include a strong regard for privacy, individual solutions to family matters, and a view of women as subordinate to men. In rural areas, men are often viewed as strong and independent power holders (Ferraro, 1983). The long-range impact of socialization and intergenerational patterns of oppression weaves victimization through the fiber of family relationships. Traditional gender roles and victimization of women are evident in the following case history of a family referred for child welfare services in a rural Appalachian county.

Mrs. Z

Married in their teens, Mr. and Mrs. Z were reared in adjacent hollows in central Appalachia. Having experienced physical and sexual abuse in early adolescence, Mrs. Z had lived in foster homes during her early teens. By age 22, she had four healthy children. Born at home, the babies had been delivered by a local midwife. Crowded into three rooms, Mr. Z assaulted Mrs. Z physically and verbally. Drinking, swearing, and wife-beating became daily happenings. Mrs. Z never questioned Mr. Z's role as head of the family, as provider, and as a source of family identity and values. Illiterate and addicted to alcohol, Mr. Z eventually died of liver disease at age 54. Mrs. Z died of cancer two years later. Cared for by her children in the absence of medical care, she died as she had lived—victimized and powerless.

The lives of each of their children took different routes. Tommy, the eldest, followed in the footsteps of his dad. He died violently from a shot fired in a physical struggle with his wife whom he had threatened to kill. He was perceived by the community as having died in the midst of "sowing his wild oats." Lucy, a frightened youngster who dropped out of school at age 14, moved into the home of her maternal grandmother, where she became intensely involved in a fundamentalist religious sect. Her involvement in the church, her sewing, and her devotion to her grandmother met with strong approval in the small community. Larry, the third child, attended school through the eleventh grade, then enlisted for military duty. He later married a "local girl" and moved into the valley not far from his childhood home. He was repeatedly arrested for drunken driving and assaultive behavior, including wife-beating. Susan, the fourth child, helped by her counselor and social worker, eventually completed college. Today, she teaches in a public high school not more than two hours driving distance from where she grew up. Viewed by the small community as "uppity," Susan rarely visits her hometown, seldom speaks of her family, and volunteers at a shelter for battered women.

For many rural women, the impact of victimization by poverty and violence has led to immobilization. The following case example reflects the strength and determination that can be mobilized by a rural Appalachian woman when she is helped to experience empowerment as an alternative to oppression.

Mrs. AA

At age 14, Mrs. AA was traded for two cows and a pitchfork to a man who was 40 years her senior. Isolated by mountains and bridgeless creeks, a ramshackle hut that had once been a chicken coop became her home. Here, without indoor plumbing, she reared three biological children and two stepchildren. Handmade bunks, a table, a radio, four straight chairs, and boxes for storage filled the one-room dwelling. Monthly visits to the country store (when she walked more than 2 miles behind her husband) were her only contacts outside her shanty home. She suffered violent beatings from her husband throughout her early childbearing years.

At age 40, Mrs. AA's plight was recognized by a school counselor when this mountain woman joined her only daughter in the freshman class at the local school. Her motivation came from fear that her husband, age 80, would die and leave her alone in the mountain shack. No longer afraid of physical violence from the hands of her elderly and frail husband, Mrs. AA declared her independence. She assumed responsibility for her aged and dependent husband and moved the family from the mountain shack. Her social worker (the first author) provided and arranged emotional and financial support during the move and throughout months of adjustment to apartment living (control). Reflection activities were used to help Mrs. AA connect meaning to her life in town with that of her former, isolated existence (existential realization). She described herself as "feeling like I am searching for something every day, something I can't have." When asked what she would have if she had her dream fulfilled, Mrs. AA replied, "I'd be a nurse" (hope). Confronted by the question, "And why can't you be a nurse?" Mrs. AA thoughtfully replied, "I guess I'll just be a nurse one day now" (hope). Having a new sense of self and direction in life (existential realization), Mrs. AA completed high school and enrolled in a training program for licensed practical nurses.

After years of beatings and poverty, Mrs. AA transcended both the gender oppression and the economic deprivation of her earlier years. Her need for affiliation was met through her own productivity in education and in work (control). Presently, she works as a nurse in a convalescent facility. Her uniform is crisp, her smile quick; only her timidity in casual conversation and a cheekbone scar belie her confidence and serve as testimonials to her former life of brutality and oppression. Her transcendence has been achieved by her giving care to countless numbers of elderly in a large nursing home (existential realization). She administers care to each in a kindly and loving fashion, a type of tender care that she has rarely experienced herself, even during her childhood and early marriage.

Mrs. AA explained her years of subservience and mistreatment. She reported that at the time she had felt powerless to change her life because she had felt entrapped by poverty, dependent upon the welfare system, obligated to follow her husband's wishes, and desirous of fulfilling the role of an obedient wife as other women in her family had done. For her, power in the family shifted when her elderly husband became frail and dependent upon her. The irony in Mrs. AA's story is that the inner strength that eventually empowered her to extract herself from isolation, poverty, and physical battering was the same force that had enabled her to endure the many years of abuse and poverty during much of her married life. Mrs. AA's story exemplifies human motivation to find meaning in life through transcending her own hardships and pain to give to others that which she never received.

Mrs. BB: A Victim of Rape and Abuse

Mrs. BB was referred for social work services by her minister for nightmares and flashbacks that terrified her and triggered crying spells, sleep problems, and sexual problems. She started experiencing these terrifying memory fragments soon after her oldest daughter turned nine years old. In her terrifying flashbacks, Mrs. BB had a recurring image of an older man who was "doing bad things to me." She reported that she had started drinking at night to put herself to sleep. She also wanted to withdraw from her responsibilities, lacked energy, and was very uncomfortable when her husband tried to initiate sex. She was having trouble going to work and no longer enjoyed her job. Mrs. BB scored 86 on the Crumbaugh and Maholick *Purpose in Life Test* (Crumbaugh and Maholick, 1966) at the end of her first clinical interview, which was a good indication that she was suffering from an existential vacuum along with her post-traumatic stress disorder symptoms. A PIL score of 92 or less indicates the presence of an existential vacuum; a score of 112 or above indicates a sense of purpose and meaning in life; a score of 93 to 111 indicates the subject is vulnerable to the development of an existential vacuum.

Mrs. BB remained in social work treatment from 1984 to 1987. During treatment she was able to remember (cleansing) that when she had been nine years old, the man who lived next door to her and her family had started molesting her by making her perform oral sex and taking photographs of her while he was molesting her. Mrs. BB remembered the man telling her that he would kill her parents if she told what was happening to her. She remembered that the man would kill small animals in front of her to show her what he would do to her parents if she ever told. The man also told her that it was her fault he was molesting her because she made him lose control and that she was evil and dirty because of this.

Mrs. BB remembered that she had told her parents what had happened to her when she was ten years old, and soon after the man moved and left the area. She remembered that her parents had taken her to their family doctor, but that nothing else had happened and "no one did anything."

Mrs. BB, her husband, and her social worker all believed that it was important for her to "remember it all and tell people about it." For Mrs. BB it was important to go to the police and file a complaint 19 years after she had been molested and abused (cleansing and control). It was important for her to talk to her parents (cleansing) about why they never did anything, to find out that her parents had no idea of what to do at the time, and that they had received no help from their family doctor who advised them to "ignore it and she will forget it sooner or later." For Mrs.

BB it was a great help when she and her husband had a second wedding ceremony (rite of initiation and cleansing). She reported that she had stopped feeling dirty after Mr. BB "proved he wanted to marry me again even after he knew what had happened to me." The couple's sex life improved dramatically after this second wedding ceremony.

A final element of Mrs. BB's therapy was her discovery that she was an excellent listener to other women who had been molested or raped. She became a volunteer at a local rape crisis center (control and existential realization) and has become a skilled volunteer counselor with other victims of trauma and terror. She also speaks to community groups about rape and assault prevention. For Mrs. BB, her volunteer work has been a way to give something to the world.

At termination in 1987, Mrs. BB's PIL score was 124, and she scored 125 on the PIL at her four-year follow-up evaluation in 1991. She reported no problems with depression, no sexual problems, and that she felt comfortable and happy. She did, however, mention that once a person learns that the world can be dangerous, "she is forever changed and has a responsibility to do something to make the world better." In our opinion, Mrs. BB has transformed the experience of being raped as a child into meaning through self-transcendent giving to the world "in honor of my sisters who have also been molested, raped, terrorized, and disempowered."

Conclusion

The broad scope of feminist literature makes it impossible to present feminist theory through a single lens. Instead, the flow of theories informing feminist social work practice provides a framework enhancing purpose in life and reducing the risk of entering a meaning vacuum. Meaning vacuums are filled by despair, confusion, anomie, depression, anxiety, substance abuse, compulsive behavior, and a loss of personal power (Lantz and Lantz, 1992). In a feminist approach to social work practice, women clients are helped to experience meaning and purpose in life, even in the face of patriarchal social structures, personal oppression, or severe physical and sexual abuse.

According to Braverman (1986), women are socialized to care for others, connecting caretaking to self-esteem, or to deriving a sense of meaning in life from being affiliated with others. In instances of rejection or loss of relationships, women may be in great danger of losing their usual way of discovering and accepting meaning. The challenge to the social worker in feminist practice is to help women experience new ways of discovering meaning.

In today's culturally pluralistic society, minority women have been said to have gained particular strength from their struggle against discrimination and oppression (Aguilar and Williams, 1993). Social workers in feminist practice cannot treat only evident social, economic, or political needs, but must have the goal of helping clients seek to transcend personal and political oppression in the power struggle of the sexes. Only by overcoming oppression can women experience true human dignity.

CHAPTER TWELVE

Elderly Clients

Understanding the existence of older people as they live in the world potentially holds great wisdom for our diverse culture and has scarcely been explored. Each society's elderly are part of the diversity in the whole configuration of the world (Frankl, 1988). A cross-sectional bit of the world's elderly encapsulates for the moment a global sense of experience from significant points in decades past. One example is World War II veterans around the world who share a common configuration and form a quilt of international memory. Their collective memory is a synthesis of globally historical moments viewed through ethnically and culturally informed lenses common to individual experiences of being in the world.

In addition to a worldwide collective memory, the world's elderly share commonalities of the biological processes of aging and anxieties that stem from the existential uncertainty of life. For many, this uncertainty triggers a sense of meaninglessness, confusion, anxiety, and depression. For those approaching the end of the life cycle, normal aging processes are often accompanied by loss of predictability and direction in life. Many elderly sense frustration in their purpose in life and lack of role fulfillment as they grow older in a changing world (Richardson, 1993).

A major challenge to social workers and other professionals who work with elderly clients is to avoid the common view that persons over age 65 represent a homogeneous population (Richardson, 1993). Instead, it is essential that the diversity of persons over age 65 be respected. In the United States, the elderly population differs by age, class, race, ethnicity, sexual orientation, religion, political preference, wellness, and lifestyle. Those elderly who immigrated to America from China, Japan, Greece, South America, Poland, Ireland, Italy, Germany, or Vietnam have vastly different roots. Elderly persons from these groups experience cross-cultural demands differently and view accepting assistance or professional help from very different perspectives (Taeuber, 1990). Interestingly, the elderly's perspectives and approaches to meaning in life in the rich, culturally diverse population of the United States varies by birthplace and the degree to which cultural assimilation or accommodation has occurred.

To view old age as a malady that is culturally prescribed negates the integrity of the human spirit (Keith, 1982). Being old in different cultures carries culturally prescribed ways of making and discovering meaning. If growing old is to be understood cross-culturally, the study of aging cannot be isolated from the cultural context in which it occurs. Nevertheless, beliefs and practices associated with ethnicity and culture need to be explored at both group and individual levels so that individual meaning potentials can be better understood. In their research with multi-ethnic elderly, Cantor, Brennan, and Sainz (1994, p. 126) remind their reader of ". . . the importance of status and differences when working with minorities of culture, rather than merely relying on ethnic differences in norms and values as such." Each culture prescribes age-appropriate social roles and generally provides transitional experiences from one role to another. Often this role transition results in meaning disruption as daily practices and familiar routines change in response to advancing age (Lantz, 1993).

Myths to Be Dispelled

Bass, Kutza, and Torres-Gil (1990) note that several myths about the elderly must be dispelled if the needs of the elderly are to be met in the years to come. First, the myth that all older persons have the same needs negates recognizing the many differences in this diverse and growing population. Second, many believe that the elderly have adequate income and retirement benefits now and will not experience inequality in years to come. Those who disagree believe that there is evidence that buying power will tend to decrease and that persons will work longer in an effort to sustain economic independence (McGuiness, 1989). Third, it is a myth that intergenerational conflicts will inevitably occur as younger persons work to provide benefits for older persons. The fourth myth is that services for the elderly need to be standardized and administered only on a national basis, as opposed to a more local basis where individual need for services becomes a primary factor of service provision at the neighborhood level. Finally, the myth that certain elderly ethnic groups are more likely to be supported by intergenerational kinship systems is possibly dispelled by research establishing very strong linkages between income and need with varying relative support (Cantor, Brennan, and Sainz, 1994). In other words, economic security provided by intergenerational systems is declining.

Myths surrounding the needs of the elderly evolve from an accumulation of life experiences and fears of unknown things to come. The fact that more persons will be living longer presents a bittersweet realization for young and old alike. Greater understanding of the needs of the new elderly, the generation about ready to exit midlife in the first decade of the twenty-first century, is necessary if the needs of the increasing proportion of elderly are to be met in years ahead (Torres-Gil and Kmet, 1990; Cantor, Brennan, and Sainz, 1994).

Common Approaches for Viewing the Aging Process

Commonalities of aging processes cut across cross-cultural boundaries of various racial and ethnic populations. Disengagement theory (Havighurst and Albrecht, 1953), continuity theory (Atchley, 1972), development theory (Sheehy, 1982), and activity theory (Maddox, 1963) are four approaches that have frequently been used to explain and predict the phenomena of aging. The most serious flaw in both continuity and disengagement theory is the omission of meaning. Both theories have been described as occurring in a "phenomenological and ethnomethodological desert" (Clark, Pelham, and Clark, 1988). It may be that many approaches to aging will become moot if the future of the world's elderly should hinge on entitlement versus productivity in response to economic necessity in a constrained market (Moody, 1990).

Disengagement theory assumes that over time the relationship between an aging individual and society is one of withdrawal.

From this approach, disengagement will inevitably occur, is universal, and is intrinsic to human nature and society. Disengagement theory is no longer viewed with great enthusiasm by many social workers who understand that older people generally remain active in everyday life, depending upon physical well-being, rather than withdrawing as they grow older (Clark, Pelham, and Clark, 1988; Hancock, 1990).

Continuity theory assumes that activities continue throughout life and that adults will maintain social involvement well into retirement. The continuity of the relationship between the aging person and society is protected as familiar roles are maintained or redefined to accommodate diminished activity without loss of self-esteem (Lantz and Lantz, 1989).

Development theory recognizes lifespan development and asserts that individuals develop new roles, activities, and interests as they pass developmental milestones. Often alternate lifestyles develop in response to role change such as those that occur in retiring. A study by Guttman (1984) confirms that many retirees find dignity in maintaining professional skills and interests well into old age. Retired persons frequently apply existing knowledge in less intensive yet meaningful ways.

Activity theory suggests that successful aging means keeping active, extending middle-age years and activities, and remaining socially and emotionally involved (Maddox, 1963; Crandall, 1980). In other words, there is often a direct correlation between high activity levels and success in aging.

The new elderly of the next decade have the potential to bring new meaning to the phenomenon of cultural diversity in a multi-ethnic society. Diversity in the United States has become part of the mainstream and is inclusive of all ages. Within the diverse population of elderly, many will be poor, some will be older or dependent, many will be productive, and some will remain as members of disadvantaged minority groups. Moody (1990) calls attention to the debate of entitlement versus productivity as a continuing, value-laden concern that holds some response to demands from social, political, and economic changes awaiting America's elderly in the coming years. Social and economic changes that are on course for aging America may well be the greatest social movement of the twenty-first century. Regardless of diversity or of their shared worldview, or lack thereof, this new aged group might well be understood from the perspective of entitlement versus productivity. Costs for the growing population of elderly are being confronted as pension incomes, social security benefits, and health care benefits take on new definitions and policies.

Changes in current attitudes toward entitlement and productivity of the elderly population will be partially shaped by verbal and educated graying people who wish to direct their own destiny. It appears that "aging" may be redefined to match the social and economic order of the world and of the United States. Change will evolve at a slower pace and will be less stressful if stigma is not attached to entitlement and if economic survival does not depend on productivity. Many conditions of aging are socially constructed and define the length of worklife, define retirement as a form of entitlement, and call for moderate to no participation in production by the elderly. Toynbee admitted that the older he became, the more he "suffered from change" (Lipski, 1984).

Just as many elderly in the past have experienced a loss of meaning by being forced into early retirement, so may today's young and middle-aged adults be forced into productivity during their "retirement" years. Such extended productivity may contribute to a meaning vacuum for those elderly who look forward to leaving jobs and who have prepared for retirement but who may lose the option to relax in their "golden" years. In situations of changed life plans such as lack of control and loss of autonomy in an area as important as working or not working at the end of the life cycle, great feelings of helplessness and meaningless are likely to be experienced through depression and other emotional or somatic dysfunctions. Loss of autonomy at the end of the life cycle is particularly overwhelming for those who have experienced lifetimes of wins and losses, changes and sameness, physical and social stresses, accompanied by work status and social network changes.

Minority and majority populations of elderly alike share in potential loss of meaning in their lives as they distance younger generations in age and values. Living alone, being separate, perhaps moving into care facilities are activities which have the capacity to destroy the potential for discovering meaning in the older years. Anglo American elderly struggle to fulfill the culturally established expectation of independence, retirement, and self-sufficiency (Green, 1995). Far too often these elderly experience great disappointment and lose their potential for discovering meaning when they encounter isolation, poverty, and loneliness away from family and friends.

There are great similarities in the process of aging, yet many culturally defined differences. Each ethnic minority group has socially constructed definitions of aging, being old, and valued or expected roles for their elderly family members. Some of these culturally defined differences are evidenced among minority groups in the American culture. African American elderly, Native American elderly, and Asian elderly are three groups who define roles and caregiving of elderly somewhat differently even in the amalgam of American society.

African American Elderly

African American elderly enjoy respect for their experiences in life and are often close to their religious and family networks. Despite the jeopardies of being old, black, poor, and often in need of medical care, the African American elderly maintain social involvement with friends, families, and "fictive kin" (Chatters, Taylor, and Jackson, 1986). African American elderly frequently maintain a kinship network that includes persons from early affectionate relationships, often from some earlier struggle to overcome severe oppression.

Native American Elderly

"The essence of Indian elderhood is grandparenting" (Green, 1995, p. 234). Older women perform many parenting duties for their grandchildren and free younger women to be economically productive. This intergenerational caregiving is a means of teaching culture, values, respect, and communication. Meaning in life is realized through intergenerational communities and purpose in family living.

Asians

Strong ethnic ties are important to Chinese elderly who look forward to the prestige that is to come with old age and will logically follow the authority and respect gained through lifelong family solidarity (Allison and Geiger, 1993). Practices of patrilineal authority, avoidance of shame, respect for elders, and religious practices celebrating ancient legends and ancestors contribute to respect for elderly Chinese (Locke, 1992; Wong, 1982). For some Chinese families, the elder relative lives in the familiar ethnic community and apart from successful children who have moved to suburban or more upscale living. Green (1995) notes that immigrant Chinese parents find their familiar ethnic community much more supportive than the isolation of suburban living.

Japanese American elderly have the wisdom of the Issei generation's participation in America, of education for the Nisei generation, and the sacrifice for the success of this younger generation through education and hardwork. The eldest son, charged with the responsibility of caring for his parents, can expect support from his brothers but not his sisters who, in turn, have in-laws with the same expectations.

Vietnamese Americans face many problems of adjustment, particularly as they age and experience isolation due to strong ethnic ties that may be less important to their sons and daughters whose American preferences formed quickly (Tran, 1988). Disempowerment and loss of ancestral roots are very painful for aging Vietnamese. Aging women lack community involvement and domestic roles in kinship systems. Green (1995) notes that "real ethnographic insight and understanding" are missing for this recent population of migrants.

The Changing Demography of America's Aging Population

Being old in America is an increasingly important matter. In 1990, one of eight Americans was age 65 or older. By the year 2050, the elderly will represent one of five Americans. Americans who are 65 or older number about 31.6 million. Of this group,

2.6 million are African American, 1.1 million are Hispanic, and 500,000 to 600,000 are of other races. It is projected that the elderly population will more than double by the year 2050, when it is expected to total 68.5 million (Taeuber, 1990). The burst in growth of this population is expected to occur when the baby boomers become 65. This will occur between 2011 and 2030 (McGuiness, 1989).

Various changes are likely to accompany this rapid increase in America's elderly. Men are expected to enjoy longer life expectancies, more women will have their own retirement pensions, education will be higher, and more elderly are expected to be productive into age 70 and above (McGuiness, 1989). Presently, elderly women outnumber elderly males by 3 to 2.6. In 1986, white women lived longer than white males, 79 to 72 years, as contrasted with African American women, 74 years, and African American men, 65 years (Taeuber, 1990).

Along with increasing life expectancy, reasonably good health is experienced by 85 percent of the generation that is older than 65 (McGuiness, 1989). Ninety percent of those age 85 or older need little assistance within their immediate surroundings, and only 25 percent of those 85 or older experience any of the dementia associated with the aging process (Jarvik, 1990).

Being elderly and retired is often accompanied by fixed incomes, including social security and pension benefits. Higher poverty rates have been identified as correlating positively with increased age. For example, of African American women above 85 years of age who lived alone in 1979, 73 percent were poor (Taeuber, 1990). Although some poverty indicators suggest that nearly 88 percent of today's elderly live above the poverty level, many elderly who live at or near the level of poverty have not been counted (Hancock, 1990). Rising costs in health care, nursing home care, and housing entail high costs that many elderly are not able to afford. Many families assist in providing these basic commodities for the increasing population of elderly, even though it is an economic hardship to do so. Societal and community-based support systems are lacking. This suggests that development at the level of primary prevention has been neglected, instead of enhancing wellness through primary prevention by assuring quality of life for the elderly. Treatment of disorders, rather than their prevention, has generally been the single focus of social work and the related helping professions (Hancock, 1990).

Stereotypes of "disengaged, senile, set in their ways, and useless" are beginning to fall away from today's elderly. The graying of America in the near future will limit discrimination and neglect of older persons. There will be diminished support for mandatory retirement and less emphasis upon age; fewer young and beautiful advertisements for cosmetic and high-fashion products; fewer bland observer or dependent roles in the few scripts portraying older characters in movies and in television serials; and fewer ageist slurs, such as arthritis, wrinkles, and graying hair jokes. The unrealistically low level of social security or supplemental income locking many elderly into poverty is another form of age discrimination (Hulme, 1984).

It must be fully recognized that the diversity of the mass of elderly includes a full range of capacities, resources, values, ethnic and racial backgrounds, religion, family structures, life experiences, losses, and need for assistance. Even though all of humanity is on the same "exit" course, individual response to aging is reactive to the nuances of each person's life experience along the way (Richardson, 1993).

Caregiving to the Elderly

At one point or another along the trajectory of advancing age, many of the elderly will experience chronic illness, widowhood, physical frailty, or deterioration in psychological functioning. Caring for the dependent elderly in a growing population of elderly is a major national concern ill-provided for in our market economy and pushed aside as an undefined task for family members. Improved nutrition, health care, and lifestyle have increased life expectancy, and debilitating aspects of aging are being delayed well into older ages for many. At least three-fourths of dependent elderly live outside institutional care systems. In 1982, 1.2 million disabled elderly were generally being cared for by families, with wives, daughters, or daughters-in-law typically being the primary caregivers (Sapp, 1984).

Despite the concern of modern families, the extended family system of caregiving is failing. Sapp (1984) makes the point that technological American society separates the family. Being shielded from the full circle of life, children and young adults are robbed of early linkages to the existential understandings of growing old and dying. Given longer life expectancy and the range of chronic disability, many families called upon to take care of a relative may find themselves to be ill-prepared, both economically and emotionally (Sapp; Lantz and Lantz, 1989).

The literature generally reflects the costs of caregiving as financial loss, depression, anger, role overload, intergenerational struggles, family disruption, and loss of employment. In both minority and majority populations, the burden of caregiving falls most heavily upon female family members (Harper, 1990a; Riemenschneider and Harper, 1990). Caretakers who suffer the most often have few societal supports and limited financial resources to use in purchasing other types of care, including respite for themselves (Sapp, 1984).

It is important to recognize that family caregivers are overburdened. Advocacy is needed to increase levels of care, including alternative care, such as day treatment programs, community-supported nursing homes, and well-equipped and affordable institutional care for dependent elderly who are in need of total care. There could be staff-supported units for elderly couples who wish to remain together but who are unable to live without skilled care, home teams to enable elderly to remain in their own homes, and adaptive equipment to make living at home possible for elderly who need help ambulating or opening a medication bottle. The environmental and equipment needs of the elderly cannot be ignored in the years to come. Furthermore, aging with dignity needs to become a protected, meaningful voyage for all persons (Lantz and Lantz, 1989).

Wellness and Independence of Elderly

The well elderly are those persons who have aged naturally and experienced no major loss of health. They have made successful adjustments to social, psychological, and economic losses. The well-being of the elderly is contingent upon not only their physical strength but also their linkage to financial, medical, and recreational support systems.

Loss associated with aging is a series of normal, but painful, episodes that occur throughout the lifespan. Illness, injuries, divorce, and failed hopes can disrupt meaning in ordinary daily routines. Identifying potentially meaningful adaptations and seeking ways to fill any meaning vacuum can restore a sense of meaning and purpose in life for the elderly just as for those who are generations younger (Lantz and Harper, 1988; Lantz and Lantz, 1989; Guttman, 1984; Hancock, 1990; Richardson, 1993).

Dependent Elderly

The dependent elderly are often physically disabled, frequently having more than one chronic disorder. Many dependent elderly become poor because of the high cost of health care. The actual number of dependent elderly is unknown, but about 5 percent of those aged 65 or older live in institutions and another one in five has a serious chronic illness (Hancock, 1990). Social work is often the profession at the interface of the dependent elderly person, extended family, and health care system. The social worker may serve many network intervention functions in situations of illness such as heart disease, mental illness, diabetes, cancer, or other serious disorders. Network intervention occurs as resources are pooled to facilitate a range of care, including medical, hospital, nursing home, home health care, hospice care, and grief counseling for the patient and for family members. Medical science has equipped providers for the level of care needed by most dependent elderly; ironically, society's valuing of the dependent elderly has not kept pace with such technological progress.

Elderly persons are often viewed as being frail, unproductive, and poor. These stereotypes are reactions to the lack of value given to elderly persons in America and to the projective fears of the viewer who is afraid of becoming the brunt of his or her own labeling behavior upon reaching old age. The diversity of the aged requires cross-culturally competent practitioners to gain awareness of their own biases and values. Social work and other helping professions can maximize the assessment of strengths and prevent discriminatory practices by working with aging clients from a wellness model of human nature (Lantz and Pegram, 1989). When elderly clients experience a meaning vacuum as they become unable to create or discover meaning in their world, they may fill this vacuum with confusion or depression, and may even lack the will to live. Their ability to create and discover meaning may be encumbered by illness, frailty, the onset of Alzheimer's disease, or the deaths of other elderly who have long been friends or family members. It is the social worker's responsibility to facilitate a reflection on life to recover meaning awareness and enhance meaning-making capacities, even to the extent of transcendence over fear and loss associated with nearing the end of life (Lantz and Lantz, 1989).

A Case Illustration: Mr. J

Mr. J, a seventy-four-year-old African American male, was referred for social services by his physician. He had recently been diagnosed as having Alzheimer's disease. Mr. J had forgotten his last name. On his "intake" day, he had somehow driven the family car to the clinic.

Mr. J was pleasant and seemed to have no understanding of why his physician was worried about him. He commented, "I know the man on your door but I can't seem to remember his name. Do you know the man on the door?" The stranger in question that particular holiday season was Santa Claus.

Mr. J, a retired coal miner, was becoming a management problem for his wife, his only caretaker. The couple was childless, but did have friends who visited regularly. Mr. J could no longer be trusted to light his pipe, do small chores around the house, go outdoors, or take a bath alone. Several community resources assisted with transportation and meal preparation. Volunteers and friends provided respite for Mrs. J by assisting with supervising Mr. J. His condition deteriorated rapidly and, unfortunately, Mr. J had to be placed in a nursing home. Visited daily by his wife, Mr. J died six months after entering the nursing home, a little less than 10 months after he failed to recognize "the man on the door."

Existential reflection and realization experiences had provided some benefit to Mr. J, both as an outpatient client and eventually as a nursing home patient. Such reflection included comments and questions to him about nature, weather, birds, objects in view, and sometimes about persons who came to his memory. Mr. J found meaning in the social pleasure gained from conversation and from the sounds of laughter. For him, meaning could only be immediately experienced. He enjoyed social exchanges, made eye contact, and liked to be joined in watching cartoons on television. Mr. J welcomed his friends into his life, forgetting their names but not the "feeling" of their relationships. Finally, unaware of his surroundings and unable to recognize his wife, Mr. J was still always less agitated during her daily bedside vigils.

Social work treatment was effective in helping Mrs. J to cope with her husband's progressive illness and in curbing the existential vacuum from which she suffered and experienced. Mrs. J experienced crying episodes, weight loss, sleeplessness, and periods of severe fatigue. She worried about being alone, and said that her house felt empty and that she did not want to face life alone. Upon being asked by the social worker how long she and Mr. J had been in love, Mrs. J replied, "Forever. Since we were just young'ens." Mrs. J wanted to be reminded that forever lasts beyond a lifetime and that she would always have Mr. J's love, just as he used to tell her. Existential realization-reflection experiences helped Mrs. J to gain the necessary strength to cope with her fears and grief during her husband's last weeks of life.

Mrs. J experienced considerable loss as reality slipped away from Mr. J, but held onto meaning from her recollection of their many years together. After his death, the life narrative method of existential reflection and realization was used to help her keep a sense of meaning in her life and in her memory of her husband. She was able to find meaning even in the pain of his illness and of his dying. Mrs. J felt that her husband would have wanted her to help others like him. A few months after her husband's death, she began to volunteer to help Alzheimer's patients and their families. She found meaning and purpose in life by giving to others some of the kindnesses that had been given to her during her time of near despair. She dedicated her helping of others to the memory of her husband.

Mrs. J and the Curative Factors

For Mrs. J, the worker's willingness to join her "emotionally" in her deep despair was the most important curative factor. Mrs. J believed that the worker had joined her world through the worker's empathy. Such empathy is the most meaningful way to demonstrate worldview respect. Catharsis-cleansing experiences occurred in response to the worker's active empathy and the worker's emotional understanding triggered hope. Network intervention and social service supports helped Mrs. J feel a greater sense of control. An additional method used by Mrs. J to process and manage her grief was the existential realization experiences she received in her volunteer work.

Conclusion

Gaining competence in cross-cultural social work practice with the elderly demands a deep awareness of professional values and biases. The helping relationship between the worker and the elderly client can be disrupted by several forces. First, worker bias and prejudice toward the elderly can impede the worker's ability to be an effective cross-cultural social work practitioner. Second, the social values that American society holds regarding its elderly impact the design of the caregiving system and reflect priorities and biases of the population at large. Third, advocacy for the needs of the aging requires that young adults and professionals confront their own mortality and look for meaning throughout the full cycle of life. Finally, the debate of entitlement versus productivity, rather than quality of retirement, results from economic concerns rather than the belief that life is meaningful so long as the human spirit is present (Frankl, 1959, 1988).

There are many coping strategies commonly used by adults in search of direction and power over their own existence. Such strategies are employed by the elderly as well (Harper, 1990). In an effort to reduce existential anxieties in the face of losing control over one's existence, or the quality of one's existence, an individual will often seek submission to religion or some greater power; abide by secular structures and systems; follow a powerful leader and protector; and seek power and control over others (Lipman-Blumen, 1984).

The motivation to search for greater meaning and purpose in life in the face of extreme odds is perhaps the greatest force of all (Frankl, 1959). In our view, a cross-cultural approach to helping must identify the defiant capability within the human spirit to overcome the limitations of the body, psyche, and environment (Frankl, 1967; Popielski, 1990). This strength of the human spirit can surpass undue hardship even in situations where the end of the human life seems inevitable (Frankl, 1959). Self-transcendence can be attained as the human spirit's potential for fulfillment is met throughout all stages of the life cycle (Frankl, 1959; Harper, 1990a).

Epilogue

The cross-cultural and special populations presented in this volume reflect a need for effective cross-cultural social work helping relationships. Cultural beliefs and practices, as well as individual differences, contribute to variations in individual response in the search to find meaning and purpose in life. Regardless of cultural orientation, the human need to experience a sense of meaning in life is the greatest single motivating force of humankind (Beranos, 1937; Day, 1952; Frankl, 1959). This common human need crosses all boundaries of diversity. Despite the human endeavor to discover meaning, the social construction of the potential to experience meaning opportunities is culturally constrained. Each person's opportunities for meaning discovery are influenced by the cultural practices and social influences in her or his present life situation and by values gained from previous life experiences (Frankl, 1959; Lantz, 1987; Harper and Lantz, 1992).

Existential philosophers point out that finding meaning and purpose in human existence is a central concern of all humanity (Frankl, 1988; Marcel, 1963). Human nature does have great homogeneity. Physical, psychosocial, developmental, and spiritual dimensions of human nature have universal elements (Frankl, 1975). Helping another human being to find meaning opportunities and potentials in everyday life, while respecting individual diversity, constitutes the core of our approach to cross-cultural social work practice.

Not unlike the diverse nature of the populations to be served, social workers, too, are diverse in their knowledge, values, life experiences, and approaches to the processes of helping others to discover and experience a sense of meaning and purpose in life. Values, attitudes, and orientation to meaning awareness are created within the cultural context of each person's life experience

(Frankl, 1988; Lantz and Harper, 1991). Cross-cultural curative factors are treatment processes common to many clients in a variety of cultural settings. Identified as helpful regardless of the client's class, ethnic background, gender, race, socioeconomic status, or age; curative factors identified in the anthropology literature and uncovered through "naturalistic research" touch the core of common human needs and the human potential to discover meaning in the world. Worldview respect, hope, helper attractiveness, control, rites of initiation, cleansing experiences, existential realization, and physical intervention are cross-cultural curative factors helpful to clients and compatible with social work practice methodologies.

This book is intended to increase the cross-cultural competence of the social work practitioner who brings personal knowledge of human difference and human need to the experience of reading this book. Consistent with generalist practice, cross-cultural social work from a curative factors perspective offers empowerment through finding meaning in living one's life and in experiencing one's own strength of being. Students and professionals alike can benefit from the practice of social work in their approach with diverse groups. The message at the core of this book is that humankind must be empowered to discover meaning in each life experience at every stage of living in the cultural configuration of the immediate world. Such empowerment may well be the key to the survival of the human race.

References

Abramovitz, M. (1988). *Regulating the Lives of Women.* Boston: South End Press.

Allison, M. T., & Geiger, C. W. (1993). The Nature of Leisure Activities among the Chinese-American Elderly. *Leisure Sciences,* 15, 309–319.

Andrews, E. (1974). *The Emotionally Disturbed Family.* New York: Jason Aronson.

Anonymous. (1990). *Reflections on a Lesbian's Experience in Therapy with a Male, Heterosexual Therapist.* Unpublished manuscript.

Appalachian Regional Commission. (1985). A Region of Contradictions. *Appalachia,* 18, 7–11.

Aquilar, M. A., & Williams, L. P. (1993). Factors Contributing to the Success and Achievement of Minority Women. *Affilia,* 8, 410–424.

Atchley, R. (1972). *The Social Forces in Later Life.* Belmont, CA: Wadsworth.

Atkinson, D., Morton, G., & Sue, D. (1989). *Counseling American Minorities.* Dubuque, IA: William C. Brown.

Attneave, C. (1969). Therapy in Tribal Settings and Urban Network Intervention. *Family Process,* 8, 192–210.

Attneave, C. (1982). American Indians and Alaska Native Families; Emigrants in their Own Land. In M. McGoldrick, T. Perce, & T. Giordano (Eds.), *Ethnicity and Family Therapy.* New York: The Guilford Press.

Atwood, J. (1992). The Field Today. In J. D. Atwood (Ed.), *Family Therapy: A Systemic-Behavioral Approach.* Chicago: Nelson-Hall Publishers.

Banks, J. A. (1987). *Teaching Strategies for Ethnic Studies.* Boston: Allyn and Bacon.

Bass, S., Kutza, E., & Torres-Gil, F. (1990). *Diversity in Aging.* Glenview, IL: Scott, Foresman and Company.

Batteau, A. (1983). *Appalachia and America.* Lexington, KY: University Press of Kentucky.

Becerra, R. (1988). The Mexican American Family. In C. Mindel, R. Habenstein, & R. Wright (Eds.), *Ethnic Families in America.* New York: Elsevier.

Berg, I., & Jaya, A. (1993). Different and Same: Family Therapy with

Asian-American Families. *Journal of Marital and Family Therapy,* 19, 31–38.

Berg, I., & Miller, S. (1992). *Working with the Problem Drinker.* New York: W. W. Norton.

Bernanos, G. (1937). *The Diary of a Country Priest.* New York: Carroll and Graf.

Billingsley, A. (1968). *Black Families in America.* New York: Prentice-Hall.

Billingsley, A. (1969). Family Functioning in the Low-Income Black Community. *Social Casework,* 50, 563–572.

Blake, W. M., & Darling, C. A. (1994). The Dilemmas of the African American Male. *Journal of Black Studies,* 24, 409–415.

Blanchard, E., & Unger, S. (1977). Destruction of American Indian Families. *Social Casework,* 58, 312–314.

Bloch, J. (1968). The White Worker and the Negro Client in Psychotherapy. *Social Work,* 13, 36–42.

Bonavia, D. (1980). *The Chinese.* New York: Lippincott and Crowell.

Braverman, L. (1986). Reframing the Female Client's Profile. *Affilia: Journal of Women and Social Work,* 1(2), 30–40.

Brende, J., & Parson, E. (1985). *Vietnam Veterans: The Road to Recovery.* New York: New American Library.

Bromley, M. (1987). New Beginnings for Cambodian Refugees—or Further Disruptions. *Social Work,* 32, 236–239.

Brower, I. (1980). Counseling Vietnamese. *Personnel and Guidance Journal,* 58, 646–652.

Brown, A. (1981). Duality, The Need to Consider this Characteristic when Treating Black Families. *The Family,* 8, 88–89.

Brown, C. (1965). *Manchild in the Promised Land.* New York: Signet.

Brown, L. (1989). Lesbians, Gay Men and Their Families: Common Clinical Issues. *Journal of Gay and Lesbian Psychotherapy,* 1, 65–77.

Burgess, N. J. (1994). Gender Roles Revisited: The Development of the "Woman's Place" among African American Women in the United States. *Journal of Black Studies,* 24, 391–401.

Burgos-Ocasio, H. (1996). Understanding the Hispanic Community. In M. Julia (Ed.), *Multicultural Awareness in the Health Care Professions.* Needham Heights, MA: Allyn and Bacon.

Campbell, J. (1983). The Southern Highlands and the Southern Highlander Defined. In B. Ergood & B. Kuhre (Eds.), *Appalachia: Social Context Past and Present.* Dubuque, IA: Kendall/Hunt Publishing Company.

Cantor, M. H., Brennan, M., & Sainz, A. (1994). The Importance of Ethnicity in the Social Support Systems of Older New Yorkers: A Longitudinal Perspective (1970 to 1990). *Journal of Gerontological Social Work,* 22, 95–128.

Carkhuff, R., & Pierce, R. (1967). Differential Effects of Therapist Race and Social Class upon Patient Depth of Self-Exploration in the

References

Initial Clinical Interview. *Journal of Counseling Psychology*, 31, 632–634.

Caudill, H. (1963). *Night Comes to the Cumberlands*. Boston: Little/ Brown.

Chan, S. (1986). Parents of Exceptional Asian Children. In M. K. Kitano & P. C. Chinn (Eds.), *Exceptional Asian Youth* (36–53). Washington, DC: ERIC.

Chatters, L. M., Taylor, R. J., & Jackson, J. S. (1986). Aged Blacks' Choices for an Informal Helper Network. *Journal of Gerontology*, 41, 94–100.

Chestang, L. (1972). Character Development in a Hostile Environment. *Social Work*, 17, 100–105.

Chung, E. (1996). Asian Americans. In M. Julia (Ed.), *Multicultural Awareness in the Health Care Professions*. Needham Heights, MA: Allyn and Bacon.

Clark, W., Pelham, A., & Clark, M. (1988). *Old and Poor*. Lexington, KY: Heath and Company.

Coles, R. (1968). *The South Goes North*. Boston: Little/Brown.

Congress E., & Lyons B. (1992). Cultural Differences in Health Beliefs: Implications for Social Work Practice in Health Care Settings. *Social Work in Health Care*, 17, 81–96.

Crandall, R. C. (1980). *Gerontology: A Behavioral Sciences Approach*. Reading, MA: Addison-Wesley.

Cravens, R. B., & Bornemann, T. H. (1990). Refugee Camps in Countries of First Asylum and the North American Resettlement Process. In W. H. Holtzman & T. H. Bornemann (Eds.), *Mental Health of Immigrants and Refugees*. Austin: University of Texas Press.

Criswell, G. (1991). The Silent Warrior. *Voices*, 27, 102–111.

Crumbaugh, J., & Maholick, L. (1966). *Purpose in Life Test*. Murfreesboro, TN: Psychometric Affiliates.

Curry, A. (1964). The Negro Worker and the White Client, A Comment on the Treatment Relationship. *Social Casework*, 45, 25–29.

Davis, L. E., & Proctor, E. K. (1989). *Race, Gender and Class*. Englewood Cliffs, NJ: Prentice Hall.

Day, D. (1952). *The Long Loneliness*. New York: Harper and Row.

de Anda, D., & Riddel, V. (1991). Ethnic Identity, Self-Esteem and Interpersonal Relationships among Multiethnic Adolescents. *Journal of Multicultural Social Work*, 1, 83–98.

de Beauvoir, S. (1968). *The Second Sex*. New York: Modern Library.

de Shazer, S. (1991). *Putting Differences to Work*. New York: W. W. Norton.

Deloria, V. (1969). *Custer Died for Your Sins*. New York: Avon Books.

Devore, W. (1983). Ethnic Reality: The Life Model and Work with Black Families. *Social Casework*, 64, 525–531.

Dixon, S. (1979). *Working with People in Crisis*. Columbus, OH: Merrill.

Dixon, S., & Sands, R. (1983). Identity and the Experience of Crisis. *Social Casework,* 64, 223–230.

Donovan, J. (1987). *Feminist Theory.* New York: The Ungar Publishing Co., Inc.

DuBois, B., & Miley, K. (1992). *Social Work: An Empowering Profession.* Boston: Allyn and Bacon.

Eisenstein, Z. (1984). *Feminism and Sexual Equality.* New York: Monthly Review Press.

Eliade, M. (1964). *Shamanism.* London: Routledge and Kagen.

Ergood, B., & Kuhre, B. (1983). Demographic Characteristics of the Region. In B. Ergood & B. Kuhre (Eds.), *Appalachia: Social Context Past and Present* (2nd edition). Dubuque, IA: Kendall/Hunt Publishing Company.

Ergood, B., & Kuhre B. (Eds.). (1991). *Appalachia: Social Context Past and Present* (3rd edition). Dubuque, IA: Kendall/Hunt Publishing Company.

Erikson, I. (1976). *Everything in its Path.* New York: Simon and Schuster.

Everett, F., Proctor, N., & Cartnell, B. (1983). Providing Psychological Services to American Indian Children and Families. *Professional Psychology,* 14, 588–603.

Fabry, J. (1979). The Noetic Unconscious. *International Forum for Logotherapy,* 2, 8–12.

Fabry, J. (1980). *The Pursuit of Meaning.* New York: Harper and Row.

Falicov, C. J. (1982). Mexican Families. In M. McGoldrick, J. K. Pearce, & J. E. Giordano (Eds.), *Ethnicity and Family Therapy* (134–163). New York: The Guilford Press.

Ferraro, K. (1983). Rationalizing Violence. *Victimology: An International Journal,* 8, 203–212.

Figley, C. (1990). *Helping Traumatized Families.* San Francisco: Jossey-Bass.

Fitzpatrick, J. P. (1987). *Puerto Rican Americans: The Meaning of Migration to the Mainland.* Englewood Cliffs, NJ: Prentice-Hall.

Frankl, V. (1953). Logos and Existence in Psychotherapy. *American Journal of Psychotherapy,* 7, 8–15.

Frankl, V. (1959). *Man's Search for Meaning.* New York: Simon and Schuster.

Frankl, V. (1962). Psychiatry and Man's Quest for Meaning. *Journal of Religion and Health,* 1, 93–105.

Frankl, V. (1967). *Psychotherapy and Existentialism.* New York: Simon and Schuster.

Frankl, V. (1973). *The Doctor and the Soul.* New York: Vintage Books.

Frankl, V. (1975). *The Unconscious God.* New York: Simon and Schuster.

Frankl, V. (1988). *The Will to Meaning.* New York: New American Library.

Freeman, J. (1984). *Women, A Feminist Perspective*. Palo Alto, CA: Mafield.

Friedan, B. (1986). *The Second Stage*. New York: Summit Books.

Garland, D., & Escobar, D. (1988). Education for Cross Cultural Social Work Practice. *Journal of Social Work Education*, 24, 229–241.

Glaser, B., & Strauss, A. (1967). *The Discovery of Grounded Theory*. Chicago: Macmillan.

Gonzalez, G. (1991). Hispanics in the Past Two Decades, Latinos in the Next Two: Hindsight and Foresight. In M. Sotomayor (Ed.), *Empowering Hispanic Families: A Critical Issue for the '90s* (1–19). Milwaukee, WI: Family Service America.

Goodtracks, J. (1973). Native American Non-Interference. *Social Work*, 18, 30–34.

Green, J. (1995). *Cultural Awareness in the Human Services*. Boston: Allyn and Bacon.

Green, R. (1989). *Homecoming: When the Soldiers Came Home from Vietnam*. New York: Putnams.

Greene, R. R., Kropf, N. P., & MacNair, N. (1994). A Family Therapy Model for Working with Persons with AIDS. *Journal of Family Psychotherapy*, 5, 1–20.

Greenlee, R. (1990). The Unemployed Appalachian Coal Miner's Search for Meaning. *International Forum for Logotherapy*, 13, 71–75.

Greenlee, R., & Lantz, J. (1993). Family Coping Strategies and the Rural Appalachian Working Poor. *Contemporary Family Therapy*, 15, 121–137.

Gregory, I., & Smeltzer, D. (1977). *Psychiatry*. Boston: Little/Brown.

Grier, W., & Cobbs, P. (1969). *Black Rage*. New York: Bantam Books.

Guttman, D. (1984). Logophilosophy for Israel's Retirees in the Helping Professions. *International Forum for Logotherapy*, 7, 18–25.

Haley, S. (1974). When the Patient Reports Atrocities, Specific Treatment Considerations of the Vietnam Veteran. *Archives of General Psychiatry*, 30, 191–196.

Hall, M. (1978). Lesbian Families: Cultural and Clinical Issues. *Social Work*, 23, 380–385.

Halleck, S. (1971). Therapy is the Handmaiden of the Status Quo. *Psychology Today*, 4, 30–34.

Hancock, B. (1990). *Social Work with Elderly People*. Englewood Cliffs, NJ: Prentice Hall.

Hanmer, J., & Statham, D. (1989). *Women and Social Work*. Chicago: Lyceum Books.

Hardy, K. (1990). The Theoretical Myth of the Same: Critical Issues in Family Therapy Training. In G. Saba, B. Karrar, & K. Hardy (Eds.), *Minorities in Family Therapy*. Binghamton, NY: Haworth.

Harper, K. (1981). Energy in Rural America: A Coming Challenge to Social Work. In J. Davenport & J. Davenport (Eds.), *The Human Side of Energy*. Laramie, WY: University of Wyoming Press.

Harper, K. (1983). Energy in Rural America. *Human Services in the Rural Environment,* 8, 24–26.

Harper, K. (1986). Appalachian Families: Aspects of Working with Developmentally Disabled Members. In A. Riemenschneider (Ed.), *Parent-Professional Interaction.* Columbus, OH: Ohio State University College of Social Work.

Harper, K. (1990a). Meaning and Midlife Crisis, A Logotherapy Approach. *The International Forum for Logotherapy,* 13, 76–78.

Harper, K. (1990b). Power and Gender Issues in Academic Administration. *Affilia,* 5, 81–93.

Harper, K. (1991). Gender Issues in Academic Administration, A Second Look at Positions of BSW Directors. *Affilia,* 6, 58–71.

Harper, K. (1992). Intervention in Cultural Confusion of Relocated Children. In B. Locke and M. Egan (Eds.), *Fulfilling Our Mission: Rural Social Work in the 1990s.* Morgantown, WV: Morgantown, The Rural Social Work Caucus and West Virginia Chapter of NASW.

Harper, K. (1996). Culturally Relevant Health Care Service Delivery for Appalachia. In M. Julia (Ed.), *Multicultural Awareness in the Health Care Professions.* Needham Heights, MA: Allyn and Bacon.

Harper, K., & Greenlee, R. (1989). Promise and Poverty in Appalachia's Heartland. *Human Services in the Rural Environment,* 13, 42–47.

Harper, K., & Greenlee, R. (1991). Workfare Program in Rural America: Joblessness in Ohio's Appalachian Counties. *Journal of Sociology and Social Welfare,* 18, 71–85.

Harper, K., & Shillito, L. (1991). Groupwork with Bulimic Adolescent Females in Suburbia. *Social Work with Groups,* 14, 43–56.

Harper, K. V. (1974). Appalachia: A Way of Life. In F. S. Riddle (Ed.), *Appalachia: Its People, Heritage, and Problems.* Dubuque, IA: Kendall/Hunt Publishing Co.

Harper, K. V., & Lantz, J. (1992). Treating Cultural Confusion in the Relocated Rural Child. *Social Work in Education,* 14, 177–183.

Havighurst, R., & Albrecht, R. (1953). *Older People.* New York: Longmans and Green.

Hayes-Bautista, D. E., & Chapa, J. (1987). Latino Terminology: Conceptual Bases for Standardized Terminology. *American Journal of Public Health,* 77(1), 61–68.

Ho, M. (1976). Social Work with Asian Americans. *Social Casework,* 57, 195–210.

Ho, M. (1990). *Intermarried Couples in Therapy.* Springfield, IL: Charles Thomas.

Holmes, R. (1991). Alcoholics Anonymous as Group Therapy. *International Forum for Logotherapy,* 14, 36–41.

Hsu, F. (1970). *Americans and Chinese.* Garden City, NY: Doubleday.

Hulme, W. (1984). Quality Aging. *Journal of Religion and Aging,* 1, 53–62.

Jaggar, A. (1983). *Feminist Politics and Human Nature.* Totowa, NJ: Rowman and Allanheld.

Jarvik, L. (1990). Role Reversal: Implications for Therapeutic Intervention. *Journal of Gerontological Social Work,* 15, 23–24.

Jilek, W. (1974). *Salish Indian Mental Health and Cultural Change.* Toronto: Holt, Rinehart and Winston.

Jilek, W. (1982). *Indian Healing: Shamanic Ceremonialism in the Pacific Northwest Today.* Laine, WA: Hancock House.

John, R. (1988). The Native American Family. In C. Mindel, R. Habenstein, & R. Wright (Eds.), *Ethnic Families in America.* New York: Elsevier.

Jones, L. (1983). Appalachian Values. In B. Ergood & B. Kuhre (Eds.), *Appalachia: Social Context Past and Present* (2nd edition). Dubuque, IA: Kendall/Hunt Publishing Company.

Jones, R. (1983). Increasing Staff Sensitivity to the Black Client. *Social Casework,* 29, 419–425.

Jue, S. (1994). Psychosocial Issues of AIDS Long-Term Survivors. *The Journal of Contemporary Human Services,* 75, 324–332.

Julian of Norwich. (1966). *Revelations of Divine Love.* London: Penguin.

Kahn, S. (1994). *How People Get Power.* Washington, DC: National Association of Social Workers Press.

Kayal, P. M. (1994). Communalization and Homophile Organization Membership: Gay Volunteerism before and during AIDS. *Journal of Gay and Lesbian Social Services,* 1, 33–57.

Kaye-Kantrowitz, M. (1992). *The Issue Is Power: Essays on Women, Jews, Violence and Resistance.* San Francisco: Aunt Lute Books.

Keefe, S. (Ed.). (1988). *Appalachian Mental Health.* Lexington, KY: The University Press of Kentucky.

Keefe, S., Reck, U., & Reck, G. (1991). Family and Education in Southern Appalachia. In B. Ergood & B. Kuhre (Eds.), *Appalachia: Social Context Past and Present* (3rd edition). Dubuque, IA: Kendall/Hunt Publishing Company.

Keith, J. (1982). *Old People as People.* Boston: Little, Brown and Company.

Kim, Y. O. (1995). Cultural Pluralism and Asian-Americans: Culturally Sensitive Social Work Practice. *International Social Work,* 38, 69–78.

Kinzie, J., & Fleck, T. (1987). Psychotherapy with Severely Traumatized Refugees. *American Journal of Psychotherapy,* 41, 82–94.

Kirk, J., & Miller, M. (1986). *Reliability and Validity in Qualitative Research.* Beverly Hills, CA: Sage.

Kitano, H. (1988). The Japanese American Family. In C. Mindel, R. Haberstein, & R. Wright (Eds.), *Ethnic Families in America.* New York: Elsevier.

Krestan, J., & Bepko, C. (1980). The Problem of Fusion in the Lesbian Relationship. *Family Process,* 13, 277–289.

Krill, D. (1969). Existential Psychotherapy and the Problem of Anomie. *Social Work,* 14, 33–49.

Krill, D. (1978). *Existential Social Work.* New York: Free Press.
Lantz, J. (1974). Existential Treatment with the Vietnam Veteran Family. In *Ohio Department of Mental Health Yearly Report.* Columbus, OH: Ohio Department of Mental Health.
Lantz, J. (1975). *Relationship Enrichment Needs of Gay and Lesbian Couples: A Phenomenological Study.* Unpublished paper.
Lantz, J. (1978). *Family and Marital Therapy.* New York: Appleton-Century-Crofts.
Lantz, J. (1986). Family Logotherapy. *Contemporary Family Therapy,* 8, 124–135.
Lantz, J. (1987). The Use of Frankl's Concepts in Family Therapy. *Journal of Independent Social Work,* 2(2), 65–80.
Lantz, J. (1989). Meaning in Profanity and Pain. *Voices,* 25, 34–37.
Lantz, J. (1990). Existential Reflection in Marital Therapy with Vietnam Veterans. *Journal of Couples Therapy,* 1, 81–88.
Lantz, J. (1991). Franklian Treatment with Vietnam Veteran Couples. *Journal of Religion and Health,* 30, 131–138.
Lantz, J. (1992). Meaning, Nerves and the Urban-Appalachian Family. *Journal of Religion and Health,* 31, 129–139.
Lantz, J. (1993). *Existential Family Therapy.* Northvale, NJ: Jason Aronson, Inc.
Lantz, J. (1994). Mystery in Family Therapy. *Contemporary Family Therapy,* 16, 53–66.
Lantz, J. (1995). Frankl's Concept of Time: Existential Psychotherapy with Couples and Families. *Journal of Contemporary Psychotherapy,* 25, 135–144.
Lantz, J., & Greenlee, R. (1990). Existential Social Work with Vietnam Veterans. *Journal of Independent Social Work,* 5, 39–52.
Lantz, J., & Harper, K. (1988). Logotherapy and the Hypersomatic Family. *International Forum for Logotherapy,* 11, 107–110.
Lantz, J., & Harper, K. (1989). Network Intervention, Existential Depression and the Relocated Appalachian Family. *Contemporary Family Therapy,* 11, 213–223.
Lantz, J., & Harper, K. (1990). Anomic Depression and the Migrating Family. *Contemporary Family Therapy,* 12, 153–163.
Lantz, J., & Harper, K. (1991). Using Poetry in Logotherapy. *The Arts in Psychotherapy,* 18, 341–345.
Lantz, J., & Lantz, J. (1989). Meaning, Tragedy and Logotherapy with the Elderly. *Journal of Religion and Aging,* 5, 43–51.
Lantz, J., & Lantz, J. (1991). Franklian Treatment with the Traumatized Family. *Journal of Family Psychotherapy,* 2, 61–73.
Lantz, J., & Lantz, J. (1992). Franklian Psychotherapy with Adults Molested as Children. *Journal of Religion and Health,* 31, 297–307.
Lantz, J., & Lenahan, B. (1976). Referral-Fatigue Therapy. *Social Work,* 21, 239–240.
Lantz, J., & Pegram, M. (1989). Cross Cultural Curative Factors and Clinical Social Work. *Journal of Independent Social Work,* 4, 55–68.

Lantz, J., & Pegram, M. (1990). Casework and the Restoration of Meaning. *Social Casework,* 70, 549–555.

Lather, P. (1991). *Getting Smart, Feminist Research and Pedagogy with/ in the Postmodern.* New York: Routledge.

Lee, D. (1976). *Valuing the Self: What We Can Learn from Other Cultures.* New York: Prentice Hall.

Lee, D., & Saul, T. (1987). Counseling Asian Men. In M. Scher, M. Stevens, G. Good, & G. Eichenfield (Eds.), *Handbook of Counseling and Psychotherapy with Men.* Beverly Hills, CA: Sage.

Lewis, R., & Ho, M. (1975). Social Work with Native Americans. *Social Work,* 20, 379–382.

Lifton, R. (1973). *Home from the War.* New York: Simon and Schuster.

Lincoln, Y., & Guba, E. (1985). *Naturalistic Inquiry.* Beverly Hills, CA: Sage.

Lindy, J. (1988). *Vietnam: A Casebook.* New York: Brunner-Mazel.

Linton, R. (Ed.). (1963). *Acculturation in Seven American Indian Tribes.* Gloucester, MA: Peter Smith.

Lipman-Blumen, J. (1984). *Gender Roles and Power.* Englewood Cliffs, NJ: Prentice Hall.

Lipski, A. (1984). Toynbee's Frantic Quest for Survival. *Journal of Religion and Aging,* 1, 47–61.

Locke, D. (1992). *Increasing Multicultural Understanding.* Beverly Hills, CA: Sage.

Loewenstein, S. (1980). Understanding Lesbian Women. *Social Casework,* 61, 29–38.

Lukas, E. (1981). Validation of Logotherapy. *International Forum for Logotherapy,* 4, 116–125.

Lyon, G. (1990). *Come a Tide.* New York: Orchard Books.

MacPherson, M. (1984). *Long Time Passing: Vietnam and the Haunted Generation.* New York: New American Library.

Maddox, G. L. (1963). Activity and Morale: A Longitudinal Study of Selected Elderly Subjects. *Social Forces,* 42, 195–204.

Majer, J. (1992). Assessing the Logotherapeutic Value of 12-Step Therapy. *International Forum for Logotherapy,* 15, 86–89.

Marcel, G. (1963). *The Existential Background of Human Dignity.* Cambridge, MA: Harvard University Press.

Mason, B. (1985). *In Country.* New York: Harper and Row.

May, R., & Yalom, I. (1984). Existential Psychotherapy. In R. J. Corsini (Ed.), *Current Psychotherapies.* Itasca, IL: F. E. Peacock Publishers, Inc.

McGuiness, C. (1989). *Aging in America.* Washington, DC: Congressional Quarterly.

McNew, J. A., & Abell, N. (1995). Posttraumatic Stress Symptomatology: Similarities and Differences between Vietnam Veterans and Adult Survivors of Childhood Sexual Abuse. *Social Work,* 40, 115–126.

McQuade, S. (1989). Working with Southeast Asian Refugees. *Clinical Social Work Journal,* 17, 162–176.

Midgley, J. (1991). Social Development and Multicultural Social Work. *Journal of Multicultural Social Work,* 1, 85–100.

Miller, W. (1982). *Dorothy Day.* New York: Harper and Row.

Min, P. (1988). The Korean American Family. In C. Mindel, R. Haberstein, & R. Wright (Eds.), *Ethnic Families in America.* New York: Elsevier.

Mirande, A. (1985). *The Chicano Experience: An Alternative Perspective.* Notre Dame, IN: University of Notre Dame Press.

Miyamoto, F. (1939). *Social Solidarity among the Japanese in Seattle.* Seattle: University of Washington Press.

Molina, R., & Franco, J. (1986). Effects of Administrator and Participant Sex and Ethnicity on Self-Disclosure. *Journal of Counseling and Development,* 63, 160–162.

Montero, D. (1979). *Vietnamese Americans: Patterns of Resettlement and Socioeconomic Adaptation in the U.S.* Boulder, CO: Westview.

Moody, H. (1990). The Politics of Entitlement and the Politics of Productivity. In E. Bass, E. Kutza, & F. Torres-Gil (Eds.), *Diversity in Aging.* Glenview, IL: Scott, Foresman and Company.

Moon, B. (1990). *Existential Art Therapy: The Canvas Mirror.* Springfield, IL: Charles C. Thomas Publisher.

Moore, J., & Pachon, H. (1985). *Hispanics in the United States.* New York: Little/Brown.

Moses, A., & Hawkins, R. (1982). *Counseling Lesbian Women and Gay Men.* Columbus, OH: Charles Merrill.

Mwanza. (1990). *Afrikan Naturalism.* Columbus, OH: Pan Afrikan Publications.

Myers, L. (1988). *Understanding an Afrocentric World View: Introduction to an Optimal Psychology.* Dubuque, IA: Kendall/Hunt Publishing Company.

Nagel, J., & Snipp, M. (1993). Ethnic Reorganization: American Indian Social, Economic, Political, and Cultural Strategies for Survival. *Ethnic and Racial Studies,* 16, 203–235.

Nes, J., & Iadicola, P. (1989). Toward a Definition of Feminist Social Work: A Comparison of Liberal, Radical, and Socialist Models. *Social Work,* 34(1), 12–21.

Norman, E., & Dumois, A. O. (1995). Caring for Women with HIV and AIDS. *Affilia,* 10, 23–35.

Obermiller, P., & Maloney, M. (1991). Living City, Feeling Country: The Current Status and Future Prospects of Urban Appalachians. In B. Ergood & B. Kuhre (Eds.), *Appalachia: Social Context Past and Present* (3rd edition). Dubuque, IA: Kendall/Hunt Publishing Company.

Obermiller, P., & Olendick, R. (1986). Moving On: Recent Patterns of Appalachian Migration. In J. Lloyd & A. Campbell (Eds.), *The Impact of Institution in Appalachia* (2nd edition). Boone, NC: Appalachian Consortium Press.

O'Brien, T. (1969). *If I Die in a Combat Zone, Box Me up and Ship Me Home.* New York: Dell.
Olzak, S. (1983). Contemporary Ethnic Mobilization. *Annual Review of Sociology,* 9, 355–74.
Osgood, C. (1951). *The Koreans and Their Culture.* New York: Ronald Press.
Parillo, M. (1985). *Strangers to These Shores.* New York: Macmillan.
Pinderhughes, E. B. (1982). Family Functioning of Afro-Americans. *Social Work,* 27, 91–96.
Popielski, K. (1990). Universal Truths. *The International Forum for Logotherapy,* 13, 49–50.
Rich, A. (1983) Compulsory Heterosexuality and Lesbian Existence. In E. Abel & E. Able (Eds.), *Women, Gender and Scholarship.* Chicago: University of Chicago Press.
Richardson, V. (1993). *Retirement Counseling.* New York: Springer.
Ridley, C. (1984). Clinical Tx. of the Nondisclosing Black Client—A Therapeutic Paradox. *American Psychologist,* 39, 1234–1244.
Riemenschneider, A., & Harper, K. V. (1990). Women in Academia: Guilty or Not Guilty? Conflict between Caregiving and Employment. *Initiatives,* 53(2), 27–35.
Robinson, J. (1989). Clinical Treatment of Black Families: Issues and Strategies. *Social Work,* 34, 323–329.
Rogers, C. (1957). The Necessary and Sufficient Conditions of Therapeutic Personality Change. *Journal of Consulting Psychology,* 21, 99–103.
Rogler, L., Malgady, R., & Rodriques, O. (1989). *Hispanics and Mental Health: A Framework for Research.* Malabar, FL: Krieger Publishing.
Rothblum, E. (1990). Depression among Lesbians: An Invisible and Unresearched Phenomenon. *Journal of Gay and Lesbian Psychotherapy,* 1, 67–86.
Ryan, W. (1969). *Blaming the Victim.* New York: Pantheon.
Rylant, C. (1982). *When I Was Young in the Mountains.* New York: Dutton.
Sager, C., Brayboy, T., & Waxenberg, B. (1972). Black Patient, White Therapist. *American Journal of Orthopsychiatry,* 42, 415–423.
Sanchez-Ayendez, M. (1988). The Puerto Rican American Family. In L. Mindel, R. Habenstein, & R. Wright (Eds.), *Ethnic Families in America.* New York: Elsevier.
Sandner, D. (1979). *Navaho Symbols of Healing.* New York: Harcourt, Brace and Jovanovich.
Sands, R. (1986). The Encounter with Meaninglessness in Crisis Intervention. *International Forum for Logotherapy,* 9, 102–108.
Sands, R. (1991). *Clinical Social Work Practice in Community Mental Health.* New York: Macmillan.
Santiago, J. M. (1993). Hispanic, Latino, or Raza? Coming to Terms with Diversity. *Hospital and Community Psychiatry,* 44, 613.

Sapp, S. (1984). On Our Obligations to the Elderly. *Journal of Religion and Aging,* 1, 27–37.

Schanberg, S. (1980). *The Death and Life of Dith Pran.* New York: Penguin Books.

Sgroi, S. M., & Bunk, B. S. (1988). A Clinical Approach to Adult Survivors of Child Sexual Abuse. In S. M. Sgroi (Ed.), *Vulnerable Populations.* Lexington, MA: Lexington Books.

Sheehy, G. (1982). *Pathfinders: Overcoming the Crisis of Adult Life.* New York: Bantam Books.

Shernoff, M. (1984). Family Therapy for Lesbian and Gay Clients. *Social Work,* 29, 393–396.

Shillito, L. (1990). *A Socialist Feminist Model for Integrative Social Work Intervention with Female Bulimics.* Unpublished manuscript.

Silver, S. M., & Iacano, C. (1986). Symptom Groups and Family Patterns of Vietnam Veterans with Post Traumatic Stress Disorder. In C. R. Figley (Ed.), *Trauma and Its Wake.* New York: Brunner/Mazel.

Solomon, B. (1976). *Black Empowerment: Social Work in Oppressed Communities.* New York: Columbia University Press.

Sotomayor, M. (Ed.). (1991). Introduction. In *Empowering Hispanic Families: A Critical Issue for the '90s* (xi–xxiii). Milwaukee, WI: Family Service America.

Spakes, P. (1989). Reshaping the Goals of Family Policy: Sexual Equality, Not Protection. *Affilia: Journal of Women and Social Work,* 4(3), 7–24.

Spindler, G., & Spindler, L. (1971). *Dreamers without Power, The Menomini Indians.* New York: Holt, Rinehart and Winston.

Starrels, M. E., Bould, S., & Nicholas, L. J. (1994). The Feminization of Poverty in the United States. *Journal of Family Issues,* 15, 590–607.

Sue, D. (1981). *Counseling the Culturally Different: Theory and Practice.* New York: John Wiley.

Sue, D., & Sue, D. (1990). *Counseling the Culturally Different: Theory and Practice* (2nd edition). New York: John Wiley.

Szapocznik, J., & Hernandez, R. (1988). The Cuban American Family. In C. Mindel, R. Habenstein, & R. Wright (Eds.), *Ethnic Families in America.* New York: Elsevier.

Taeuber, C. (1990). Diversity, the Dramatic Reality. In S. Bass, E. Kutza, & F. Torres-Gil (Eds.), *Diversity in Aging.* Glenview, IL: Scott, Foresman and Company.

Takashima, H. (1977). *Psychosomatic Medicine and Logotherapy.* Oceanside, CA: Bebor Science Books.

Tick, E. (1989). *Sacred Mountain, Encounters with the Vietnam Beast.* Santa Fe, NM: Moon Bear Press.

Timberlake, E., & Cook, K. (1984). Social Work and the Vietnamese Refugee. *Social Work,* 29, 108–113.

Tobin, J., & Freidman, J. (1983). Spirits, Shamans and Nightmare

Death: Survivor Stress in a Hmong Refugee. *American Journal of Orthopsychiatry,* 53, 439–448.

Tomine, S. (1991). Counseling Japanese Americans: From Internment to Reparation. In C. Lee & B. Richardson (Eds.), *Multicultural Issues in Counseling: New Approaches to Diversity.* Alexandria, VA: American Association for Counseling and Development.

Tong, R. (1989). *Feminist Thought: A Comprehensive Introduction.* Boulder, CO: Westview Press.

Torres-Gil, F., & Kmet, M. (1990). Elder Leadership in a Diverse America. In S. Bass, A. Kutza, & F. Torres-Gil (Eds.), *Diversity in Aging.* Glenview, IL: Scott, Foresman and Company.

Torrey, E. (1986). *Witchdoctors and Psychiatrists.* New York: Harper and Row.

Torrey, E. (1988). *Nowhere to Go.* New York: Harper and Row.

Towle, C. (1952). *Common Human Needs.* Silver Spring, MD: National Association of Social Workers.

Tran, T. V. (1988). The Vietnamese American Family. In C. Mindel, R. Habenstien, & R. Wright (Eds.), *Ethnic Families in America: Patterns and Variations.* New York: Elsevier.

Treviño, F. M. (1987). Standardized Terminology for Hispanic Populations. *American Journal of Public Health,* 77(1), 69–72.

Tseng, W., & Hsu, J. (1991). *Culture and Family: Problems and Therapy.* New York: Haworth Press.

Tsui, P., & Schultz, G. (1985). Failure of Rapport: Why Psychotherapeutic Engagement Fails in the Treatment of Asian Clients. *American Journal of Orthopsychiatry,* 55, 561–569.

Tully, C., & Greene, R. (1994). Cultural Diversity Comes of Age: A Study of Coverage, 1970–1991. *Arete,* 19, 37–45.

Tully, C., & Nibao, J. (1979). Homosexuality, A Social Worker's Imbroglio. *Journal of Sociology and Social Welfare,* 7, 154–168.

Van Den Bergh, N., & Cooper, L. (1986). *Feminist Visions for Social Work.* Silver Spring, MD: National Association of Social Workers.

Wagner, R. M. (1993). Psychosocial Adjustments during the First Year of Single Parenthood: A Comparison of Mexican-American and Anglo Women. *Journal of Divorce and Remarriage,* 19, 121–141.

Weaver, D. (1982). Empowering Treatment Skills for Helping Black Families. *Social Casework,* 28, 100–105.

Weiner, R. (1983). Utilizing the Hispanic Family as a Strategy in Adjustment Counseling. *Journal of Non-White Concerns,* 11, 133–137.

Weiss, B., & Parish, B. (1989). Culturally Appropriate Crisis Counseling: Adapting an American Method for Use with Indochinese Refugees. *Social Work,* 34, 252–254.

Wells, K. (1995). The Strategy of Grounded Theory: Possibilities and Problems. *Social Work Research,* 19, 33–37.

Williams, C. (1983). The Mental Foxhole, The Vietnam Veteran's Search for Meaning. *American Journal of Orthopsychiatry,* 53, 4–17.

Williams, J. (1987). *Eyes on the Prize: America's Civil Rights Years.* New York: Penguin.

Wimsatt, W. (1955). *The Verbal Icon.* New York: Noonday Press.

Winbush, G. B. (1996). African-American Health Care: Beliefs, Practices, and Service Issues. In M. Julia (Ed.), *Multicultural Awareness in the Health Care Professions.* Needham Heights, MA: Allyn and Bacon.

Wong, B. P. (1982). *Chinatown: Economic Adaptation and Ethnic Identity of the Chinese.* New York: Holt, Rinehart and Winston.

Wong, M. (1988). The Chinese American Family. In C. Mindel, R. Habenstein, & R. Wright (Eds.), *Ethnic Families in America.* New York: Elsevier.

Yalom, I. (1980). *Existential Psychotherapy.* New York: Basic Books.

Index

Acculturation coping strategy, 2–24
Activity theory of aging, 142–43
African American family
 extended relationships in, 40–41
 role flexibility in, 39–40
African Americans
 adaptive technique of duality, 38–39
 community strengths, 42–43
 cross-cultural curative factors, 43–45
 discrimination against, 36–37
 diversity among, 36
 duality strategy, 38–39
 elderly, 145
 extended family relationships, 40
 problems as minority, 36–38
 role flexibility, 39–40
 self-transcendence training, 41
 victimization of, 36–37
Aging process
 common approaches to, 142
 losses associated with, 149–50
 redefinition, 144
Anomic depression
 among migrating minority people,
  74–75
 among Native Americans, 28–29
Appalachian people
 identification of, 83–84
 migration of, 74–75
 out-migration, 91–92
 response to migration, 92–95
 traditional identity, 84–86
 value system of, 86–91
Appalachian region, 84
Asian people

Asian American demographic characteristics, 60
 elderly, 145–46
 as social work clients, 61–73
 See also Chinese American clients;
  Japanese Americans; Korean Americans; Southeast Asians
Assimilation, cultural, 52–55

Biculturism. See Duality or biculturism
Black church, 42–43

Caregiving for elderly people, 148–49
Chinese American clients, 63–65
Cleansing experiences, 14–17
Clients, minority culture
 coping strategies, 22–25
Clients, minority culture
 effect of migration on, 74–75
 use of cross-cultural curative factors
  for, 21–22
Cohesion-independence issue, 119–20
Commonalities
 aging process, 142
 cross-cultural, 3–4
Continuity theory of aging, 142–43
Control as curative factor, 12–13
Coping strategies
 African American, 43
 duality strategy of African Americans, 38–39
 of minority culture clients, 22–25
 used by minority group members,
  21–22

173